john **k. white**

unafraid

walking tall along fearful paths

Mainstay Church Resources

Unafraid

Cover Illustration: Joe VanSeveren
Cover Design: Dody Antony
Interior Design and Typesetting: Dody Antony

Unless otherwise marked, Scriptures are taken from the *Holy Bible,* New Living Translation, copyright © 1996. Used by permission of Tyndale House Publishers, Inc., Wheaton, Illinois 60189. All rights reserved.

Scripture quotations marked NIV are taken from the HOLY BIBLE, NEW INTERNATIONAL VERSION ®. NIV ®. Copyright © 1973, 1978, 1984 by International Bible Society. Used by permission of Zondervan Publishing House. All rights reserved.

Scriptures marked NASB are taken from the *NEW AMERICAN STANDARD BIBLE* ®, © Copyright The Lockman Foundation 1960, 1962, 1963, 1968, 1971, 1972, 1973, 1975, 1977. Used by permission.

Scriptures marked (AMP) are taken from The Amplified Bible, Old Testament. Copyright © 1965, 1987 by The Zondervan Corporation. The Amplified New Testament, copyright © 1954, 1958, 1987 by The Lockman Foundation. Used by permission.

Scriptures marked KJV are taken from the *Holy Bible,* King James Version.

Scriptures marked CEV are taken from the *Holy Bible,* Contemporary English Version, copyright © 1995, American Bible Society.

Scriptures marked *Message* are taken from THE MESSAGE. Copyright © by Eugene H. Peterson 1993, 1994, 1995. Used by permission of NavPress Publishing Group.

Vision of Mainstay: In this sight and sound culture, our holy task is to help pastors help people grow on Sundays and beyond. To support this vision, Mainstay provides practical tools and resources, including the annual 50-Day Spiritual Adventure, the Seasonal Advent Celebration, the Month of Sundays Series, and our website: www.sundaysolutions.com.

MAINSTAY
*Leading the Team for
Life-Changing Sundays*

Printed in the United States of America
ISBN 1-57849-317-X

2003 2004 2005 2006 2007 2008 2009 2010
10 9 8 7 6 5 4 3 2 1

contents

introduction

a song for all fears

Every tomorrow has two handles;
we can take hold of tomorrow by the handle
of fear and anxiety or by the handle of faith.
—William Ellis

One author described the process of writing as a performance before two intimidating audiences. On stage left are the critics—past, present, and future—who remind you that not all readers will appreciate your effort. On stage right are the supporters who offer affirmation and encouragement yet you fear they will be disappointed.

5

"Both these groups," says the author, "form a Gestapo, and I can't shake what one writer called 'the feeling that the Gestapo is going to come to my door and arrest me for impersonating an intellectual.'"[1]

Well, that's one of my fears. Plenty of books are already available on the subject. Just "thumbing" through a popular book website revealed forty-seven titles containing the words, "Freedom from Fear" alone. So what makes this book unique? Rather than an exhaustive consideration of *fear*, or a list of simple answers for difficult situations, it's intended to be a tour guide as you trek along this 50-Day Spiritual Adventure called *Standing Tall: Facing Fears That Grip the Soul*.

In J.R.R. Tolkien's *The Hobbit,* Gandalf wants a hobbit, Bilbo Baggins, to accompany him on an adventure. Baggins replies:

> We are plain, quiet folk and have no use for adventures. Adventures . . . nasty, disturbing, uncomfortable things. Make you late for dinner, I can't think what anybody sees in them.[2]

Little did Bilbo know that many fears awaited him on that adventure. Our purpose is not to cause fear, but to discover principles from God's

Word which enable us to walk tall along fearful paths.

You will notice various references to the fascinating classic *The Lord of the Rings* throughout the book. Tolkien, an Oxford professor of English, began writing about hobbits, little people who inhabit part of an imaginary place called Middle Earth, while serving in the British army during World War I. A devout believer, Tolkien interlaced his stirring fantasy of good confronting evil with Christian themes such as sacrifice, love, fellowship, commitment, duty, temptation, grace, and forgiveness.

Though seemingly insignificant and powerless, a hobbit—Frodo Baggins, nephew of Bilbo— emerges as the hero among heroes to save Middle Earth from destruction. His commitment and courage serve to challenge every believer to stand tall against the fears that grip our souls.

Fear not! You don't have to be a Tolkien aficionado to understand this book. I'll only refer to those lovable hobbits and their friends briefly in each chapter as their experiences relate to the particular fear we are considering. But, because of what these characters can teach us about facing our fears and terrors, and because *The Lord of the Rings* trilogy has impacted my life as few other books have, it seems advantageous to learn from these adventurers during our own Adventure.

We're talking about fear: a general term defined variously as a feeling of alarm, fright, or even terror caused by the sudden or impending expectation of danger, pain, or catastrophe. Fear has always gripped the human soul. Some of the popular music titles and their artists express this apprehension: "The Fear of Being Alone" (Reba McEntire), "Fear" (Bon Jovi), "Fear of Flying" (Vitamin C), "Fear of Falling" (Badlees), "Year to Fear" (Downward Spiral), "Anguish and Fear" (Yngwie Malmsteen), "No Hope = No Fear" (Soulfly), "Fear of the Marketplace" (Neil Diamond), "Fear of the Dark" (Iron Maiden), "Hidden Fear" (Richard Wright), "Gripped by Fear" (Front 242), and on it goes.

Two kinds of fear exist: healthy and unhealthy—and actually maybe a third—let's call it *entertaining fear.* Many people love scary television shows, horror movies, haunted houses, roller coasters, frightening camping stories, Steven King-type novels or dangerous over-the-top feats. One of the top three programs amid the reality TV craze was NBC's *Fear Factor,* a nominee for best reality television series at the People's Choice Awards in 2003. Contestants agreed to face their worst fears in order to win money. America loves to watch and imagine having to face those fears themselves.

In an article entitled "Fear Factor," Christine Sneeringer discusses the world's "morbid attraction to fear." She says such programs "capitalize on our bizarre fascination with fear."[3] But why do we find fear so fascinating? Why do we like scary things? Greg Laurie proposes that it's the *perception* of terror in a controlled, safe environment—such as reading a book by the fireplace at home—that excites us.[4] So as long as we know nothing will harm us, bring it on.

Healthy fear alerts us to danger or a challenge. It motivates us to take proactive measures, such as:

* searching for the source of an electrical smell in the house,
* taking shelter when the weather siren sounds,
* seeking medical help when our body is ill or in pain,
* buckling down in our studies when we receive a low academic exam score,
* taking deep breaths and going over our notes one more time when we feel nervous before performing or speaking,
* heeding the Holy Spirit's warning about a potential disobedient decision.

Healthy fear provides the wherewithal to confront the source of apprehension head-on by making us more alert and resolute.

Unhealthy fear expresses itself in worry or anxiety. For our purposes we will regard these words as synonymous. Unhealthy fear serves as not so much an alarm signaling danger but a trap waiting to ensnare us. Byproducts of unhealthy fear include physical illness, phobias and addictions, marital and family problems, lower energy levels, reclusive lifestyles, lack of confidence, and missed opportunities for growth and service.

By way of illustration, let's use the fear of what people may think of us. The Bible says "Fearing people is a dangerous trap, but to trust the Lord means safety" (Proverbs 29:25). When we experience unhealthy fear we feel anxious and fail to put our confidence in God. We let it control or "trap" us. Healthy fear serves as an alarm reminding us to face our terror of people, knowing that the Lord's presence will strengthen us.

We can't ignore the possibility that physiological factors in a person's DNA or brain functioning intensify some fears. Troublesome phobias —a few of which are death (necrophobia), thunder and lightning (brontophobia), cancer (cancerphobia), heights (acrophobia), vomiting (emetophobia), confined spaces (claustrophobia), open spaces (agoraphobia), flying (aerophobia), people or social situations (sociophobia), and spiders (arachnophobia)—may result.

The Bible speaks many times about fear, which first emerges in the Garden of Eden when Adam says, "I was afraid because I was naked" (Genesis 3:10). The Lord gives his first command concerning fear, "Do not be afraid," to Abraham after he rescues Abraham's nephew, Lot, from the hands of four terrorist kings and promises him great blessing (Genesis 15:1).

Depending upon who's counting and in what translation, the Bible contains approximately 365–370 "fear not" statements. Perhaps the reason God comments on fear so much has to do with the power it has to make us disobedient. How comforting to know, however, that he knows our anxieties and that knowledge provides us with the spiritual resources to serve him with courage.

Although the list seems endless, we will concentrate on eight of life's fears that can be particularly troublesome in these times. Ever read the 1991 novel entitled *The Sum of All Fears,* by Tom Clancy? Well, the Bible, with much warning and counsel on the subject, has one passage in particular that we could call *A Song for All Fears* (Psalm 34), addressing all eight of these conditions:

- Terrorism and war—*For the angel of the Lord guards all who fear him, and he rescues them. . . . For the Lord protects them from harm—not one of their bones will be broken* (verses 7, 20).

- Financial insecurity—*Let the Lord's people show him reverence, for those who honor him will have all they need. Even strong young lions sometimes go hungry, but those who trust in the Lord will never lack any good thing* (verses 9–10).

- Rejection and betrayal—*The Lord is close to the brokenhearted; he rescues those who are crushed in spirit* (verse 18).

- Skeletons in the closet—*Everyone who trusts in him will be freely pardoned* (verse 22b).

- Failure and disgrace—*Those who look to him for help will be radiant with joy; no shadow of shame will darken their faces* (verse 5).

- Disease and death—*I cried out to the Lord in my suffering, and he heard me. He set me free from all my fears* (verse 6).

- Paralyzing what-ifs—*The righteous face many troubles, but the Lord rescues them from each and every one* (verse 19).

* Gathering doom—*The eyes of the Lord watch over those who do right; his ears are open to their cries for help. But the Lord turns his face against those who do evil; he will erase their memory from the earth* (verses 15–16).

We will look at this psalm throughout the book, along with many other scriptures, to help us loosen fear's grip and grasp the faith we need to walk tall along fearful paths.

1 Barbara Wright, "How I Wrote Fat Chance," *College English,* 44.3 (March 1982).
2 J.R.R. Tolkien, *The Hobbit* (Boston: Houghton Mifflin Company, 1999) 6.
3 Christine Sneeringer, "Fear Factor" *Christian Single* Oct. 2002. Online article summary "Singles Fear Not!" *Current Thoughts & Trends Page,* November 2002, <navpress.com/ctt>.
4 Greg Laurie, *Why Believe?* (Wheaton, IL: Tyndale House Publishers, Inc., 2002) 35–36.

Do not be afraid of the terrors of the night,

nor fear the dangers of the day. . . .

He guided them safely, so they were unafraid . . .

—Psalms 91:5 NLT; 78:53 NIV

chapter one

loosening the grip of
terrorism & war

*We must remember that evil does not wear a turban, tunic, a
yarmulke, or a cross. Evil wears the garment of a human heart
woven from the threads of hate and fear.*
—Nathan Baxter, dean of Washington National Cathedral

During a National Geographic television special on factors influencing J.R.R. Tolkien to
write *The Lord of the Rings,* the narrator introduced viewers to the novel by saying, "The
forces of good and evil clash in our epic battle
that will determine the course of Middle Earth.
But one small spot is isolated from the conflict,

its inhabitants blissfully unaware of the dangers beyond their fertile fields."[1]

As the adventure begins, Frodo Baggins and his friends soon become acquainted with the chilling nature of terrorism as the Black Riders seek to destroy Frodo and reclaim the Ring. Terror grips the souls of Strider and the Hobbits as shadowy, dark shapes slowly approach. Fearing for their lives, Merry and Pippin fall to the ground, and Sam clings to Frodo, shivering with terror.[2]

•••

In Tom Clancy's *The Sum of All Fears,* the young CIA analyst Jack Ryan seeks a solution to the mounting nuclear threat posed by neo-Nazi terrorists in Europe. Having found a lost Israeli nuclear bomb, the terrorists make plans to explode it at the Super Bowl and blame the scheme on Russia in order to rekindle cold war hostilities with America. Clancy describes a scenario of nuclear weapons in terrorist's hands, and suggests how quickly fears could rise and cause nations to act without thinking.[3] Reviewer Roger Ebert noted, "In these dark times, it is not a thriller but a confirmer, confirming our fears that the world is headed for disaster."[4]

Terrorism and war occupy the world's attention in this new century. No longer do we think of it in terms of occurring in Northern Ireland, Israel, or Africa, for example, but also in North America. Shortly after Gulf War II began, *USA Today* ran an article entitled "Americans muster strength to fight fear: Young get first taste of terrorism, war, civil unrest."[5] The author quoted Princeton sociologist Robert Wuthnow's concern over how new fears will affect society:

> I worry because we are a spoiled society. We are used to being consumers and having almost instant gratification. I am concerned about Americans having the courage and perseverance to deal with terrorism. . . .This is the first time my generation has had to face any real hardship. This war against terrorism has the potential to either ruin or define my generation.

The United States Department of Defense defines terrorism as "the calculated use of violence to inculcate fear; intended to cause or to intimidate governments or societies in the pursuit of goals that are generally political, religious, or ideological."[6] Countries like Canada have established extensive security initiatives since

9/11, such as an anti-terrorist act, changes in transportation security and immigration procedures, and improved border security.

As twenty-first century people, we look at common things more suspiciously. We think twice when we see white powder, check drinking water for poison, look askance at unattended bags in public places, use air travel less—but when we do travel we know not to carry box cutters, knives, scissors, screwdrivers, aerosol sprays or any number of similar items through airport security.

Frightened people in previously "safe" countries now ponder plans for building "safe rooms" in their houses and buying antibiotics and gas masks. Anxiety levels rise each time a new tape is released by terrorists, security warnings get closer to the color red, or a rogue group or nation sponsors acts of terrorism or threatens war.

Most people do not want war—I say most, because war does have positive benefits for some. During my time in Vietnam I met a number of fellow soldiers on their second or third tour. They volunteered because wartime duty looks good on your record for promotions. Others liked the extra hazardous duty pay. I had the opportunity to make the grade of Captain overnight—if I would "re-up" for one more year.

Of course, the fine print all but guaranteed one more tour of duty for me in Vietnam. I declined, respectfully. War definitely benefits those who want to advance in the military.

War also fulfills the desires of those who want to see their arduous and often monotonous training realized in combat. For example, more than once I've seen television interviews with jet fighter pilots eager to get out there and do what they are trained to do—destroy targets and, yes, kill people.

Other military personnel fee their "destiny" is to fight for glory. In the film *Patton* the egotistic yet capable general looked over a World War II battlefield strewn with bodies and commented on the thrill of battle (and uttered a brief prayer of confession).

Industry profits from war as well, especially those that manufacture arms, uniforms, equipment, supplies—anything related to supporting the wartime effort. But, for most, war is unwelcome, especially when the action takes place where we live or affects our lifestyles. Because of terrorism's upsurge, that could mean anywhere. War certainly does not benefit the wounded or killed military and civilian personnel and their loved ones. I receive a check each month in compensation for wounds received in action—it helps. But I would gladly stop receiving those payments if the battle scars could be erased.

In these early years of the twenty-first century the world increasingly fears terrorism and war. We've learned from previous hostilities that war terribly disrupts not only the groups or nations involved, but others as well. War wreaks havoc on national budgets and the financial well being of citizens. It tends to intensity prejudices against other races or ethnic groups, erode civil liberties, threaten the safety and livelihood of people from other nations living in terrorist or war regions.

Confront the unknown with confidence in the known

Terrorism and war are in our face. So, how can stand tall in faith and face these gripping fears? The customs of early Native Americans furnish us with a helpful illustration. Adult men would train young boys in survival skills such as hunting and fishing. A boy's final exam came at age thirteen when his elders took him blindfolded several miles away into the wilderness and left him for the night without food or protection. It was a fearful, even terrifying experience for the young brave-to-be, for he had never known such isolation.

Nightfall amplified normal sounds: rustling branches, cracking twigs, howling animals, noisy insects. The young man imagined all sorts of terrible dangers surrounding him—wild animals ready to pounce, or snakes or spiders sneaking up to bite.

After a seemingly endless night, his environs gradually appeared less threatening as the sun illumined the sky. Finally allowed to look around, he saw the path that led back to his tribe—and only a few feet away stood his father, armed with bow and arrow! He had provided protection for the boy throughout the night.[7]

His fears of the unknown terrorized the boy needlessly—needless because of his father's presence. One of the keys, then, to facing fears such as terrorism and war, is to *confront the unknown with confidence in the known.* The "known" is the collection of promises God has revealed to us in his Word, especially of his presence and protection when we experience life's terrors.

The setting of Psalm 34, our *Song for All Fears* mentioned in the introduction to this book, finds David on the run from King Saul (1 Samuel 20—21). Saul intended to kill the young soldier, so David said his goodbyes to his best friend Jonathan, the king's son, and headed for Nob to seek the Lord's guidance and secure provisions from the tabernacle. From there he fled to Gath, presumably to seek asylum from the Philistine King Achish. Because the king's servants recognized David as the beloved and true "king" of Israel and their enemy, David feared for his life. He feigned mental illness to prevent appearing as a threat to the king and escaped to a cave.

Two verses in this psalm relate to the fear associated with terrorism and war:

> For the angel of the Lord guards all who fear him, and he rescues them.
> For the Lord protects them [the righteous] from harm—not one of their bones will be broken! (Psalm 34:7, 20)

Note the promises of God's presence and protection to alleviate fear. His presence assures and his protection surrounds those who trust in God ("all who fear him") that nothing will happen without God's loving approval:

> For the Lord God is our light and protector. He gives grace and glory. No good thing will the Lord withhold from those who do what is right. (Psalm 84:11)

A Moravian missionary story from the annuls of memorable stories on the foreign mission field illustrates God's protection. Two pioneering missionaries went to a cannibalistic tribe to proclaim Christ's gospel. In ignorance, the tribe brutally murdered them.

Twenty years later an American missionary couple went to this same area to establish a mission station. They soon sensed the power of darkness and hostility surrounding them. The couple greatly feared for their lives night by night, yet continued to seek strength from God's word and prayer.

One day a villager came to their home and asked to see their guards. The missionary replied, "I have no watchmen, only a cook and a little boy."

The visitor asked permission to search the house but found no one else. When the missionary asked for an explanation, the man answered, "When you and your wife came here we determined to kill you as we did the missionaries twenty years ago."

We can only try to imagine the fear that gripped the missionary upon hearing these words! The villager went on to say that whenever they had approached the house to kill them at night, they always found a double row of guards, armed with shining weapons, surrounding the house. "At last we hired a professional assassin," he continued, "who said he feared neither God nor devil. Last night he came close to your house. . . .We followed at a distance. There stood the shining watchmen, and the killer fled in terror."

The man said they had given up their murderous plan, but wanted to see those guards close up and know where they came from. At this point, the missionary opened his Bible and read from our *Song for All Fears*:

> "For the angel of the Lord guards all who fear him, and he rescues them."[8]

We need to immerse ourselves in God's promises in order to face our fears unafraid. *Unafraid,* in our context, doesn't mean "without fear." It means we are trusting in our Lord for the power to stand tall in faith against the terror. The Word of God plays a key role in this story.

Unfortunately, an alarming trend exists concerning how Americans, for example, view the Bible. Researcher George Barna recently reported, "Over the past 20 years we have seen the nation's theological views become less aligned with the Bible. Americans still revere the Bible and like to think of themselves as Bible-believing people, but the evidence suggests otherwise."[9]

Is it any wonder that many westerners struggle with fear of terrorism and war to the extent that we do? The Apostle Paul records a wonderful promise:

> Can anything ever separate us from Christ's love? Does it mean he no longer loves us if we have trouble or calamity, or are persecuted, or are hungry or cold or in danger or threatened with death? . . . And I am convinced that nothing can ever separate us from his love. Death can't, and life can't. The angels can't, and the demons can't. Our fears for today, our worries about tomorrow, and even the powers of hell can't keep God's love away. Whether we are high above the sky or in the deepest ocean, nothing in all creation will ever be able to separate us from the love of God that is revealed in Christ Jesus our Lord. (Romans 8:35, 38–39)

There are seventeen possible threats in this entire passage (verses 35–39). Paul says not one of them can separate us from God's love and care. Let's look at a few; first of all, *trouble*. This word may be translated "tribulation" and means "pressure." Let's imagine we are grapes freshly picked from the vine and thrown into a large vat. Suddenly people start jumping into the vat and stomping on us. The pressure becomes too great that we are squished flat with one stomp. Ever feel like that? The word *trouble* describes the force grapes undergo in the vat as they are stomped upon. Not even crushing trouble can separate us from his love and care.

How about *calamity?* This word is variously translated "hardship" or "distress." It means "narrowness,"—that hemmed-in feeling of being squeezed by our circumstances. Calamity cannot separate us.

"Threatened with *death*." The word literally means "sword." No weapons—even of mass destruction—can separate us from God's love and care.

Of all these things and more, Paul says, "I am convinced" (absolutely persuaded). Is terrorism and war included here? You bet. We can face that fear unafraid because of his promise *never* to let *anything* separate us from his love and care for our lives. *Confront the unknown with confidence in the known.* The "known" is the promises God has revealed to us in his Word, especially of his presence and protection.

I've found that matching up a verse or passage from Scripture with the fear I'm experiencing helps bring about peace. Memorizing a verse or passage, or at least knowing where to locate it helps a great deal in finding the right portion of God's Word. The key isn't just to recite or read the verse, but to take it to the Lord as a reminder of his promise, and then to take the necessary action to face that fear by faith.

For example, let's use a verse I memorized years ago:

> Have I not commanded you? Be strong and courageous. Do not tremble or be dismayed, for the Lord your God is with you wherever you go. (Joshua 1:9, NASB)

Joshua and God's people are approaching Canaan, a land that struck terror in the hearts of the majority of spies years before (Numbers 13). Going in will mean facing terrorism and war. God knows Joshua's fear and reassures him several times of success and his presence (Joshua 1:1–9, 12–13, 15).

In verse 9, the Lord exhorts Joshua to be strong and face his fears unafraid, based on the promise of his presence. Notice what happens next:

Joshua then commanded the leaders of Israel, "Go through the camp and tell the people to get their provisions ready. In three days you will cross the Jordan River and take possession of the land the Lord your God has given you." (Joshua 1:10–11)

Joshua believes God's promise and begins to *confront the unknown* (what lies ahead in Canaan) *with confidence in the known* (God's promise). So when faced with a fearful situation we go to a verse like Joshua 1:9 and remind ourselves of his promise.

Another calming promise easily related to the fear of terrorism and war is found in Psalm 91:

Do not be afraid of the terrors of the night, nor fear the dangers of the day. . . . Though a thousand fall at your side, though ten thousand are dying around you, these evils will not touch you. . . . If you make the Lord your refuge, if you make the Most High your shelter, no evil will conquer you. (verses 5, 7, 9–10a)

During the long plane ride from San Francisco to the Republic of Vietnam, I claimed these promises in Psalm 91. I did not take God to mean he would protect me from injury or even death, but that I would be safe in his will, whatever transpired. Early on I experienced some "terrors of the night" in the form of sniper fire, incoming mortar rounds, and on one occasion, an irate water buffalo. It took two clips (40 bullets) before we stopped him from trying to trample the whole company. The "dangers of the day" (*arrows*) included patrolling in mines and booby-trapped areas, and hearing bullets fly by our heads from out of nowhere.

So when facing fear we can *confront the unknown with confidence in the known* by reminding ourselves of the promises of God we have committed to memory.

J.R.R. Tolkien paints a terrifying picture as war threatens Middle Earth. The Dark Lord, Sauron, seeks to rule all lands once he repossesses the Ring. The situation looks bleak. All must decide for or against Sauron. Life will never be the same again. Galdalf speaks with King Theoden of Rohan and encourages him to face the rising tide of terror. After some deliberation, Theoden lifts his sword and rallies his people to stand tall against this unwelcome but very real fear.[10]

Set a goal for yourself right now to memorize several verses of Scripture during this 50-Day

Adventure. Review the list of suggested passages in your journal and start working on the ones that fit the particular fears you experience. Here are a few hints I've found helpful in order to hide God's Word in our hearts:

1. Review the passage in several translations and choose the most meaningful rendition.
2. Write the passage on a 3x5 or similar card.
3. Slowly read aloud the passage five times.
4. Begin to memorize the verse or passage phrase by phrase. For example, the first phrase in Romans 8:38 is, "And I am convinced that nothing can ever separate us from his love." Work on that until you have it, then move on to the next.
5. Carry the card with you and review what you've memorized; then work on the next phrase.
6. Review your work daily until you have it down. Review, review, review. Do it while driving, walking, washing dishes—whenever. It only takes a minute or two. One of the best times for me is while swimming laps at the gym. It makes the time go faster, too!

W. Graham Scroggie, in *A Guide to the Psalms,* tells about John Fisher, who on Tuesday, June 22, 1535, walked up the wooded steps which led to the dreaded scaffolding where many bloody executions had taken place. His sick, wasted body felt strangely energized after imprisonment in the Tower of London for over a year. As Fisher climbed he quoted the words of Psalm 34:5— "They looked unto Him, and were lightened; And their faces were not ashamed" (KJV). Kneeling to receive the executioner's axe, he joyfully repeated, "In Thee, O Lord, do I put my trust" (Psalm 31:1, KJV) until death ushered him into the presence of Christ. Fearful, but unafraid.

We stand tall and face the fear of war and terrorism when we confront the unknown with confidence in the known of God's Word, "Sharper than any double-edged sword" (Hebrews 4:12, NIV).

[1] *National Geographic Beyond the Movie—The Lord of the Rings: The Fellowship of the Ring.* National Geographic, 2001.

[2] J. R. R. Tolkien, *The Fellowship of the Ring* (Boston: Houghton Mifflin Company, 1994) 190–191.

[3] *The Sum of All Fears,* dir. Phil Alden Robinson, DVD, Paramount Pictures, 2002.

4 Roger Ebert, *The Chicago Sun-Times,* 31 May 2002.

5 Karen S. Peterson, *USA Today,* 27 March 2003.

6 *Department of Defense Home Page,* <dod.gov>.

7 Dennis J. DeHaan, "Our Daily Bread."

8 A. Naismith, *A Treasury of Notes, Quotes, and Anecdotes,* (Grand Rapids: Baker Book House, 1975) 11.

9 "Large numbers of Americans view Bible, Quran as equal," 5 Feb. 2003, <www.pastors.com>.

10 J. R. R. Tolkien, *The Two Towers* (Boston: Houghton Mifflin Company, 1994) 423–424, 505–506.

Let the Lord's people show him reverence,

for those who honor him will have all they need.

Even strong young lions sometimes go hungry,

but those who trust in the Lord will

never lack any good thing.

—Psalm 34:9–10

chapter two

loosening the grip of
financial insecurity

When faced with want and when our supply is threatened,
we are on miracle territory as long as we remain
where God has placed us. . . .
And in the place of fear comes a thrilling
anticipation of God's supply—in His way, in His time.
—Joseph M. Stowell, *Kingdom Conflict*

What is the most pressing challenge or difficulty in your life?

Suze Orman, the popular personal-finance guru
and author of several books including *The Laws*

of Money, the Lessons of Life, would say it's "the rocky economy." The Barna Research Group agrees. They asked a similar question and discovered that the top personal concern is related to finances, followed by health, career, and parenting. Economic issues rated second highest (under war and terrorism) when asked about national concerns.[1]

A recent Gallup poll confirmed that Americans still regard finances as the number one personal concern. Another Gallup poll revealed that the number one long-term national worry is the economy.[2] Money makes the greatest difference in how many people respond to life.

Financial insecurity raises its worrisome head increasingly these days. Frequently we hear of layoffs or a company filing for bankruptcy and closing many of its local stores or curtailing its services. More and more names of people who need work appear on church prayer lists. The 9/11 disaster did a number on the stock market which had already become "bearish." As a result, many people nearing or at retirement age today worry about the future. People seek second and even third jobs to make ends meet or save for the future.

How much is enough?

Most of us don't necessarily want to become rich, but want "enough" (defined differently by each of us) to provide both needs and wants so we can live comfortably. If we had "enough" we wouldn't experience financial insecurity—at least, that's what we think.

USA Today, in a revealing study, asked the question, "How much does it take to become rich?"[3] Interviews revealed contrasting values and philosophies:

- A lawyer, with $1 million in investments, a $500,000 home, and the ability to take several $8000 vacations each year, said he would need another million in stocks and bonds to be "rich."
- A software developer had $2 million in cash and a $2 million home. He didn't consider himself rich and worried about a stock market crash.
- A couple with a net worth of $7 million, plus two homes, two sports cars, and a sailboat wouldn't consider themselves rich until they could purchase a $5 million personal jet so the husband could be freer for business and personal affairs.

- A financial service company's senior vice-president believed financial freedom started at $10 million.
- A successful businessman required at least $20 million in investments to keep up his $3 million yacht, $2.5 million personal jet, and $1.5 million mountain estate.
- A young multimillionaire said, "enough" for him meant twice as much as he currently had.

In his helpful book, *Financial Freedom*, Ray Linder testifies that in his own experience "enough" meant just a little more than he possessed:

> It was frustrating because there were so many different levels of so-called financial freedom. Each time I had achieved one level of success, another height beckoned. More money brought more anxieties and more entanglements. . . . Like the Sirens' sweet songs that lured Greek sailors to wreck their ships upon the rocks, the allure of just "a little more" led me on a journey that always looked great until I reached my destination.[4]

When asked, "How much money is enough?"

John D. Rockefeller replied, "Just one dollar more." No matter our situation, rich or poor or in-between, relying upon "enough" will never be enough to bring financial security.

David Broder of *The Washington Post* stated that one in seven families in the middle-income range have debts of at least 40% of their income. That's a huge amount! No wonder many of us lie awake at night worried about making ends meet. Some of these debts are genuine; some are the result of poor financial management. But sometimes how well we manage what we have gets overshadowed by conditions we cannot control. The stock market's downward trend shows no partiality.

A couple of examples are typical: One retiree spent $30,000 in what he considered a wise investment and saw it decline in recent years to only $900 in value. A former management consultant said she had faithfully followed the advice of experts in financial matters, yet lost about one-half the value of her investments.[5] These people made what they thought were wise choices in carefully managing their resources, but factors beyond their control took over.

Scams can produce financial insecurity. For example, one type on the increase is an "affinity fraud" where people within the same religious, professional, or ethnic connections are approached with "get rich quick" schemes. Such frauds play on trust and relationships that tend to quell skepticism.

Some members of The Tabernacle of Praise in Brooklyn, New York, found themselves ripped off by a group called Financial Warfare, Inc. This organization approached the pastor who, in turn, recommended the program to his church. The people placed their trust in his evaluation and in Financial Warfare because they prayed with them and even donated funds to the church. Everything seemed on the up and up, an answer to their prayers. Also, since their friends seemed convinced, some church people purchased stock that eventually lost all its value. Some who could not afford it lost many thousands of dollars.

Years ago a church I attended had the dream of building a state-of-the art health care center that would minister to the physical, emotional, and spiritual needs of the disabled and seniors. People gave excitedly with the promise of a high return on their investment. Many people placed their entire savings into the program. My wife and I invested a sizeable amount (for a seminary student) but my inborn skeptical nature held some back. We trusted our pastor and the church board, and we believed in the ministry goals.

This wonderful facility received the community's applause. Patients and residents received top-notch care, and many trusted Christ as Savior—until the money ran out. Mismanagement, extravagant spending, and an inability to pay the promised return on investment eventually caused the church to enter into receivership. The courts called it fraud. Most people, like us, were surprised and saddened that a good idea had failed, but the collapse placed many into a state of financial insecurity.

Yes, we lost some of our investment. When a letter came, asking if we would forgive the accrued interest and accept the principle, we gladly accepted the offer because we believed the leadership had sincerely attempted to do something great for the kingdom of God. Today, we regard the pastor at that time as highly as before, especially for the manner in which he and the church attempted to make restitution with as many people as possible.

Let's face it, regardless of national economic realities or scams, the way some of us manage or fail to manage our finances may cause us and others needless anxiety and grief. Some of us simply do not know how to manage money matters.

Impulsive spending, sometimes caused by unhappiness or greed, and buying expensive things to make us appear and feel more successful, usually cause financial problems.

These uncontrolled emotional "wants," even seemingly good or noble wants, can drown us in deep waters financially. As debt piles up, so does anxiety and we find that our financial problems largely govern how we make decisions about all of life. Pastor and counselor Ed Hindson writes about some of the devastating effects of financial mismanagement:

> Decisions are made hastily, and things go from bad to worse. Financial bondage usually leads to carelessness, impulse buying, speculation, and—worst of all—credit buying. Those who charge the most can usually afford the least, and their debts mount up. Getting out of debt becomes their overriding concern.[6]

Even people who normally discipline themselves in money matters are not immune to financial difficulties, especially during a shaky economy. To both groups, financial superstar Suze Orman might chime in at this point with one of her laws of money and say, "Look at what you have, not at what you had."[7] Van Thurston might say, "Praising God puts the right perspective on your problems."[8] Both would be right, but what about God—what might he say to alleviate our fears about how we're going to pay the bills, send the kids to college, afford health insurance, or even just live in the future?

What is God doing?

Joe Stowell offers five suggestions as to what God may be doing in our lives during such times:

- Tearing away self-sufficiency to prove again that He is our only true source.
- Redefining our values. As long as we trust in him, the significance of family, friends, spiritual realities, his Word, and prayer come back into focus.
- Teaching us to be resourceful and diligent with what we have.
- Giving us the opportunity to reevaluate our earning and spending habits so that slothfulness and overspending may be eliminated.
- Reminding us of the difference between needs and wants.[9]

What may God want to do in your life during this time of uncertainty? Several of my friends have experienced hard financial times over the years. As they related their stories to me, common questions they asked God were, "What am I supposed to learn from this?" or "What am I doing wrong?"

Don and Bonnie (not their real names) experienced two periods of financial stress—the first while in their thirties, and the second in their fifties. They call it the "Don and Bonnie roller coaster" as their emotions fluctuated wildly. Don describes those times as the painful process of God peeling away the layers of self to reveal the really important values in life. Both times, Don struggled with his worth as a man, which he connected with having a job. Until you find yourself unemployed, you don't really realize to what extent you equate your identity as a person with what you do or don't do for a living. It's a very lonely, depressing, and fearful experience that a growing number of men experience in these days.

Without realizing it, he also "confused security in God with the ability to make a living." God opened his eyes when the paychecks stopped coming. His greatest fear? The inability to make money and provide for the family. That's what men do and Don could no longer perform that husbandly, fatherly duty—truly a terrifying situation.

Bonnie's apprehension was not as focused as Don's on the lack of money. Because she grew up in a large family with many expenses and mediocre means, she had greater tolerance for limited funds. Her greatest fear concerned the affect this unwelcome trial was having on her husband. She anguished over his lack of contentment and fervently prayed for Don to be at peace and develop a grateful spirit.

Looking back, they describe their first experience of unemployment as an "education," and the second as an "adventure." Younger, less worried, "a time to get through" with many years still ahead, the first experience taught them, through tears and trepidation, important values and drew them closer together as a couple and family. Dad losing his job naturally upset their children. How agonizing it must have been for them to see their children alarmed and confused as they wondered what was happening to the family as they knew it. The family learned over those worrisome days, however, to see God at work providing for their needs.

The second time became an adventure with a unique set of fears. The children had grown and now the issue centered on how they would prepare for retirement, as well as live in the present.

Once again the painful process of God's removing layers of self commenced, and Don again wrestled with inner doubts as to his worth, abilities, and the insecurity and shame of no paycheck. Bonnie, too, worried about their future, and felt her husband's pain for not having a job where he could be appreciated and respected for his unique skills—even if the salary was less.

In the end, Bonnie made a fascinating observation. If she could have her choice of fears, the next time she would choose financial insecurity. Through tough times she has discovered that many things in life outrank money in importance. As to any advice for others suffering from the panic of financial insecurity, Don and Bonnie believe couples need to tackle financial problems together, rather than allowing obstacles to divide them. Instead of ignoring difficulties, couples need to ask the "what-ifs" in a positive way and plan for the future. For example, "What if Don dies; how would Bonnie pay the mortgage?" Otherwise, as Don picturesquely depicts it, worries will "unravel you like peeling an onion."

Another couple, now in their fifties, has weathered three periods of unemployment in the last ten or fifteen years. "Hank" says he remained fairly "cool" through those times. However, in the brief time I spent with Hank I sensed the tension he must have felt inside as he strenuously wrestled with fear of the future, and at the same time sought to trust his God to see them through.

The first period of unemployment totally blindsided Hank, unexpectedly hitting only days after purchasing a new car with payments. On his way home from work after hearing, "Your services are no longer needed," he wondered how he would tell Martha. A dedicated employee, Hank worked long hours. When he came home early that afternoon, Martha immediately sensed what had happened and said, "You lost your job," and gave him a hug. The layoff scared her a great deal. Facing this new and frightening experience, Martha anxiously searched until she found a better paying job in order to help boost family income.

After arduously searching for a year, going on several out-of-state interviews, a local acquaintance mentioned he had a position open. Hank's skills fit the job, but the industry and job environment were totally different and the salary came to about one-half of his wages at the former job. Glad to have found something, Hank took the job and worked hard to do well, but after about six months his employer informed him that they had found someone more qualified.

This time, both Hank and Martha felt relief more than shock. Neither of them liked the job climate in which Hank had had to work, yet the monster of unemployment was once again lifting it ugly head. During this second period of unemployment their college-bound daughter graduated from high school. They felt her recent acceptance to a Christian college was the Lord's will, so they continued her registration process, praying for the Lord to provide.

Then, at their daughter's graduation party, a childhood friend of Hank's, whom he had not seen in 10 years, invited Hank to partner with him in a new company. Shortly after the company started business, a manufacturing company offered Hank a job, again at about half the income level, but a good fit with his experience. With great relief Hank commented, "the Lord provided." This income from both jobs enabled Hank and Martha to finally make ends meet.

After a short time another position opened up in their home town. Hank readily accepted the job which would allow him and his wife to live nearer to both of their recently widowed mothers. Hank held an important position at a competitive salary, enjoyed his work, and developed good ideas for the company.

Unfortunately, when the company was sold, the new owners terminated his position. Hank has now started his own company, with a sizeable portion of his own resources. Although the company has yet to see a profit and the apprehension that reality yields, Hank and Martha steadfastly trust their living Savior to see them through.

As with Don and Bonnie, Hank and Martha acknowledge that God is teaching them to regard money and possessions as having a lesser value. Martha explains, "In the whole scheme of things, there are more important things than money," like family and other relationships. She adds that they are learning to get along with less. In some cases God simply makes things last longer, like their car with over 150,000 miles that continues to work just fine. Fearful, but unafraid.

What does God promise?

We've already been introduced to Psalm 34 (see introduction) but let's take a closer look at verses 9 through 14:

> Fear the Lord, you his saints, for those who fear him lack nothing. The lions may grow weak and hungry, but those who seek the Lord lack no good thing. Come, my children, listen to me; I will teach you the fear of the Lord. Whoever

of you loves life and desires to see many good days, keep your tongue from evil and your lips from speaking lies. Turn from evil and do good; seek peace and pursue it. (NIV)

Did you see the promise? Those who fear (reverence, be in awe of) and seek (care for, require, inquire of) the Lord will never lack good things and will see many good days (as opposed to bad days). Note the clear responsibilities David sets forth dealing with our speech and behavior:

- Keep your tongue from evil
- Keep your lips from speaking lies
- Turn from evil
- Do good
- Seek peace
- Pursue peace

Some other related promises in Scripture are:

The Lord is my shepherd; I have everything I need. (Psalm 23:1)

And this same God who takes care of me will supply all your needs from his glorious riches, which have been given to us in Christ Jesus. (Philippians 4:19)

No good thing does he withhold from those whose walk is blameless. (Psalm

84:11, NIV)

> And God will generously provide all
> you need. Then you will always have
> everything you need and plenty left over
> to share with others. (2 Corinthians 9:8)

Carefully note that these promises also contain a clear or implied expectation of responsibility on our part. The passages are summarized in the table on the following page.

The key to standing tall and facing the fear of financial insecurity is to fear the Lord by obeying his commands. Note that the last two passages in the table refer to the specific act of giving as an act of obedience. Ray Linder comments: "It took a while, but eventually I came to understand that God's Word says that financial freedom for oneself is a lie. True financial freedom comes when I use my money to acquire freedom for others instead of myself."[10]

Getting started

During days of financial hardship, the Linders, like our two couples, learned that many things in life take precedence over money. They also came to believe that whatever amount of money you now possess is "enough," if you are putting your trust in the Lord to provide.

Text	Promise(s)	Responsibility
Psalm 34:9–14	You will never lack good things and will see many good days	Fear (reverence, honor) the Lord in all speech and behavior
Psalm 23:1	You will have everything you need	Consider him your shepherd
Psalm 84:11	You won't miss any good thing	Walk blamelessly
Philippians 4:19	All your needs will be supplied	Give to the Lord's work (from 4:10–18)
2 Corinthians 9:8	You will be generously provided for	Sow generously in giving (from 9:6–7)

In Tolkien's *Lord of the Rings,* Gandalf's apparent death shocks the Fellowship, for they had depended upon him for more help than they realized. As Aragorn summons his friends to continue their journey, he holds up his sword, looks at the mountains, and says what sounds almost like a prayer: "Farewell, Gandalf! . . . What hope have we without you?"[11] When Gandalf—a type of Christ figure—later returns as a "resurrected" man, Aragorn exclaims, "Beyond all hope you return to us in our need!"[12] In any of life's matters, our hope must reside in the Lord God. He longs for us to express our need of him through prayer.

Trusting God to provide is inextricably linked to prayer. An acquintance of mine, Lynn, is a missionary who found herself "grounded" due to poor health. Discouraged over her situation, at first she tried a medical leave, but the mission eventually decided she could not return to the field. This young woman found herself in the throes of financial insecurity—no income, no savings, and little cash. She could not help but feel frightened.

Fearful but not afraid, Lynn began praying for a job and for God to show her appropriate financial objectives. One of her goals was to own a home in five years. I was intrigued by the frequent references to prayer in her life. Lynn sought prayer often from her friends, and was faithful to pray for them. In every case, God answered by meeting the need.

Lynn comments, "He continues to faithfully provide for each need. . . . An extra check comes when I have an unexpected bill; a dryer was given to me to match the washer; . . . someone called to ask if he could help insulate my attic. . . . My faith has been built up as I continue to find God to love me lavishly, revealing His intimate care for the details of life."[13] Lynn is learning the secret of contentment that the apostle Paul wrote about from a prison cell in Rome—"For I have learned to be content whatever the circumstances" (Philippians 4:11, NIV). Lynn stands tall with a firm grip on faith against the fear of financial insecurity.

Don and Bonnie shared with me that one of the keys to standing tall against fear was their prayer life. Individually and together, they would pray, oftentimes plead, for their Master to direct them as his servants for that day, knowing his love for them. Don called it something like "a daily walk, looking to the Master." This communication with God helped free them from worry.

They particularly prayed that God would "change our desires." One morning they woke up and realized God had answered this prayer.

In similar fashion, the practice of prayer continues as a way of life for Hank and Martha. Said Hank, "We just trust the Lord to provide—he always has." The following is a model prayer, called "The Unafraid Prayer," you may want to follow for the rest of the Adventure:

> *Lord, I know that when I feel afraid,*
> *you want to calm my heart.*
> *Yet, at this moment, I'm not at peace*
> *about* _____
> _____.
>
> *The enemy wants me to be consumed by*
> *this fear. But your Word reminds me:*
> (Fill in memory verse).
> *Thank you that I can face my fears*
> *unafraid, knowing you are always with me.*
> *Amen.*

Use this prayer daily. Make the words your own. Use whatever scripture fits the need, but do not fail to apply the truth of God's Word to your fear. Power and faith come when we match our fear with a promise from the Bible.

Do I sound unspiritual in saying that prayer might not be enough? Prayer is the just the beginning. Let me illustrate with a story Ed Hindson tells of a businessman whose personal finances were in shambles. "I've prayed for God's help, but I don't think even God could help me now," the man told Hindson. The problem was obvious to the counselor—the man was living way beyond his means. He had a $5000 per month mortgage, two boats, and a huge credit card debt. So Hindson informed him, "God won't help you until you get your finances in proper biblical order."[14]

As you pray for courage to face this fear, know that the Lord is vitally concerned about your situation and won't let you down. Keep in mind the things he may be doing through these circumstances to strengthen you, let him direct your choices, and be open to seeking the counsel of others to help you stand tall—fearful, but unafraid.

[1] George Barna, "Most Americans Satisfied with Life Despite Having Quality of Life Issues," *Barna Research Online,* 26 March 2002, <Barna.org>.

[2] George Gallup, Jr., *The Gallup Organization,* 22 Jan. 2003 and 16 April 2003 <Gallup.com>.

[3] Paul Davidson, "So, How Much Money Does It Take to Be Rich? *USA Today* 20–21 June: 1A–2A; cited in Ray Linder, *Financial Freedom* (Chicago: Moody Press, 1999) 12–13.

4 Ray Linder, *Financial Freedom* (Chicago: Moody Press, 1999) 13.

5 Walt Duka, "Overcoming Hard Times," *AARP Bulletin,* April 2003: 23-24.

6 Ed Hindson, *Overcoming Life's Toughest Problems* (Eugene, OR: Harvest House Publishers, 1999) 134.

7 Andrea Sachs, review of *The Laws of Money, The Lessons of Life,* by Suze Orman, *TIME* (31 March 2003): 192.

8 Van Thurston, *Hope at the Bottom* (Chicago: Moody Press, 1996) 57.

9 Joseph M. Stowell, *Kingdom Conflict* (Chicago: Moody Press, 1996) 102–103.

10 Linder 13.

11 J. R. R. Tolkien, *The Fellowship of the Ring* (Boston: Houghton Mifflin Company, 1994) 325.

12 J. R. R. Tolkien, *The Two Towers* (Boston: Houghton Mifflin Company, 1994) 484.

13 Linder 189–190.

14 Hindson 130.

I am scorned by all my enemies

and despised by my neighbors. . . .

When they see me on the street,

they turn the other way.

I have been ignored as if I were dead. . . .

—Psalm 31:10–12

chapter three

loosening the grip of
rejection & betrayal

The fear of rejection tempts us to deny who we really are
in order to succeed in our quest for acceptance and love.
—H. Norman Wright

Distraught over Frodo Baggins's absence, Sam
Gamgee rushes to the river where he finds his
master preparing to leave without him. Frodo
tells Sam he must go to Mordor alone and that
Sam would just hinder his plan to destroy the
Ring. He labels Sam a nuisance, which hurts Sam
deeply, for he is willing to give his life for Frodo.

Fortunately for Sam, Frodo changes his mind,
admitting that Sam's company would be most
comforting on this fearful journey. Frodo laments
over never again seeing the others in the
Fellowship. Sam, the ever-present encourager of
his friend says, "Yet we may, Mr. Frodo. We
may."[1]

•••

Rejection can be traumatizing. We've all experienced it. Here are some of its sounds:

- I don't like you.
- You're not what we're looking for.
- I want her on my team (not you).
- What? You didn't make the team?!
- I don't love you anymore.
- I never loved you.
- I wish you'd never been born!
- Go away, you bother me.
- I'm sorry, I have other plans.
- We wanted a boy.
- Let's just be friends.
- Your grades are better, but. . . [even straight
  A's wouldn't be good enough].
- Thank you for your interest in our position,
  but it's not a "good fit."
- No thanks, I'm not interested.
- Man, you're stupid.

There are passive rejections as well, like when:
- A friend no longer calls.
- The boss assigns more significant work to others.
- You're not invited to a meeting or social gathering.
- No one greets you at church.
- You get passed over for a promotion.
- Your opinion doesn't seem to be valued.
- You volunteer for a ministry team and never hear a word.
- Your parents seem to favor a brother or sister over you.
- You're not included in the "in group" (not necessarily bad, but it can hurt at the time).
- You rarely hear any affirmations or praise about your work or yourself.
- You're trying to make conversation with a person who keeps looking over your shoulder or around the room or at his watch, or excuses herself to talk with another person.

A painful experience in my life occurred during the transition from elementary to junior high school (sixth to seventh grades). In the sixth grade I had a special pal. We played together at recess, rode bikes home from school, played on the weekends—he was simply my best friend.

When fall came, we attended a much larger school fed by a number of area elementary schools. My friend and I ended up in different homerooms, so we didn't see each other as much. The junior high was farther from home and we went our separate ways to and from school.

But what really hurt was his decision to spend time with new friends, in and outside of school. So, the drift began and continued on through high school, and eventually a cherished friendship died. I felt terribly rejected. Of course, I made new friends as well, one with whom I still correspond today. But the hurt of abandonment at that time still stings.

Another former "best friend" incident took place during high school. We grew up together and did everything together—rode bikes, played pretend adventures, wrestled, and yes, got in trouble many times. We knew every yard—back and front—of every house on the block, and played wherever we desired, invited or not. One day we wandered into one of the neighbor's garages and found all sorts of paint. The next thing we knew, we were painting the inside of his garage—without his help or permission! (I'm telling this not from memory, but from the account told me most sternly by my parents).

One day the sad news came that my friend's dad took a job in another town. We each found new friends, but I never forgot my special pal.

As it turned out, he later moved back to town, and we attended the same high school. But things were different. We'd been apart so many years and grown up along such different paths that a once-special connection no longer sparked. The kind of friends he liked were not the kind I particularly liked and so we continued on our separate paths. What happened was natural, a common experience, but I missed the friendship, as it used to be on the block—perhaps meant to be unique only for that time. But in his love, God provided several other good friends during high school and college days.

These and other painful events during those young years taught me to fear and withdraw from possible situations where rejection might happen. I also learned that the more we get rejected, the better we get at imagining rejection, which just makes the agony worse. We learn quickly to deceive ourselves into seeing and feeling something as a rebuff. We become skillful at writing future scenarios, which cause us to panic, but few of which actually come to pass. In brief, we master the art of avoiding rejection and in doing so, we sometimes cause it to happen by presenting a negative image of ourselves to others (which we accept as torturously true).

The constant fear of rejection is literally a *dreadful* way to live. It dampens our joy, keeps us on the defensive, and inhibits the formation of meaningful ties with others. Doug Rumford helps us understand the motivations and terror of those who fear rejection:

> Some overfunction in an effort to be liked or appreciated. They think their activity will insure their acceptance. Others function in a more defensive way, carefully guarding themselves against overexposure lest someone take advantage of them. Their premise is that you cannot be rejected if you have not asked to be accepted. Whether doting or defensive, such reactions generate an anxious under-current of fear, making relationships more of a burden than a blessing.[2]

In his classic, *Why Am I Afraid to Tell You Who I Am?* John Powell cuts to the core: "If I tell you who I am, you may not like who I am, and it's all that I have."[3] Do you hear the terror? We fear that revealing the real me will not meet the other person's standards of acceptance.

So people who live with the fear of rejection often hesitate meeting new people, avoid discussing core values, or do not readily share their faith in Christ. Exposing our real selves causes too much discomfort. It just isn't worth the risk of pain that we have felt many times before.

John Ortberg offers a helpful illustration about playing "the quiet game." His parents would sometimes have the children play this game when they were being noisy—"Let's see who can be the quietest the longest." Ortberg admits that he still plays that game but for different reasons. Sometimes he won't speak up for fear of what people will think of him, or for the pain that conflict might engender, or for the energy it might take to clean up "the relational mess" his words might cause. Many of us, he says, play "the quiet game" in various ways, for example:

- When we pretend something doesn't bother us but it does.
- When we pretend to agree but don't.
- When we pretend not to care, but we do.
- When we want to hide from or avoid conflict or rocking the boat.

Ortberg asserts that the underlying issue is fear and people who play this game often end up frustrated and resentful and lose opportunities to experience "authentic intimacy."[4]

Some positive realities to remember

A look at God's Word reveals some positive realities we would do well to remember in order to loosen fear's grip on us. The first reality to remember is that *God never rejects us:*

> "The Lord is close to the broken-hearted; he rescues those who are crushed in spirit." (Psalm 34:18, NIV)

> "Even if my father and my mother abandon me, the Lord will hold me close." (Psalm 27:10,)

Out in the countryside fleeing from King Saul, David must have felt rejection, not only by Saul, but even the Lord at times. On another occasion, David faced an extremely evil conspiracy that caused even his friends to ostracize him. Listen to the pain in these words of rejection (all):

> I am scorned by all my enemies and despised by my neighbors—even my friends are afraid to come near me. When they see me on the street, they turn the other way. I have been ignored as if I were dead, as if I were a broken pot. (Psalm 31:11–12)

Those who hate me without cause are more numerous than the hairs on my head. . . . For I am mocked and shamed for your sake; humiliation is written all over my face. Even my own brothers pretend they don't know me; they treat me like a stranger. . . . Their insults have broken my heart and I am I despair. If only one person would show some pity; if only one would turn and comfort me. (Psalm 69:4,7–8, 20)

But now hear his belief in God's acceptance of him (all):

Praise the Lord, for he has shown me his unfailing love. He kept me safe when my city was under attack. In sudden fear I had cried out, "I have been cut off from the Lord!" But you heard my cry for mercy and answered my call for help. (Psalm 31:21–22)

For the Lord hears the cries of his needy one; he does not despise his people who are oppressed. (Psalm 69:33)

The writer of Hebrews quotes two Old Testament passages that speak of confidence in relationship to God (Deuteronomy 31:6 and Psalm 119:6–7):

> God has said, "Never will I leave you;
> never will I forsake you." So we say with
> confidence, "The Lord is my helper; I
> will not be afraid. What can man do to
> me?" (Hebrews 13:5b–6)

So the first reality to remember is that *God
never rejects us.*

The second reality: *our Lord knows how rejection feels and empathizes with the brokenhearted.*
Isaiah, speaking of Messiah's rejection, wrote:

> He was despised and rejected—a man
> of sorrows, acquainted with bitterest
> grief. We turned our backs on him and
> looked the other way when he went by.
> He was despised, and we did not care.
> (Isaiah 53:3–4)

Yet, it was necessary for him to endure such
suffering in order to identify with us and become
our High Priest:

> Since he himself has gone through suf-
> fering and temptation, he is able to help
> us when we are being tempted. . . .
> This High Priest of ours understands our
> weaknesses, for he faced all of the same
> temptations we do, yet he did not sin.
> (Hebrews 2:18; 4:15).

God never rejects us. He knows the feeling of rejection, and he empathizes with the broken-hearted.

The third reality: *other people are necessary for our personal growth.* H. Norman Wright relates how the Babemba tribe in southern Africa seeks to encourage those who have been caught misbehaving in some way. The tribe places the person in the center of the village and all the people surrounded him. For as long as it takes, every person, young and old, speaks directly to the wayward villager, describing his or her strengths, good deeds, and positive traits without a word of criticism. When everyone has spoken, they welcome the person back into the tribe. The goal is to have the person experience and believe acceptance and love to such as extent that he or she will not act in such an irresponsible manner again.[5]

Many who study human behavior agree that when we try to solve problems by ourselves we get overtaken by them and end up drowning or getting beached. And yet, in order to find fulfillment it's essential to take risks. The renowned physician/psychiatrist, Paul Tournier maintained,

> No one can develop freely in this world and find a full life without feeling understood by at least one person . . . He who

> would see himself clearly must open up
> to a confidant freely chosen and worthy
> of such trust. Listen to all the conversa-
> tions of our world. . . . They are for the
> most part dialogues of the deaf.[6]

The Christian-hating terrorist we know as Paul
(called Saul at that time) discovered this truth
immediately after his conversion to Christ (Acts
9:17–18). The first person he met followed
Christ. God summoned Ananias to seek out Saul,
which he did obediently, yet with great fear. We
know this is true because Ananias had said to the
Lord, "I've heard about the terrible things this
man has done to the believers in Jerusalem! And
we hear he is authorized by the leading priests to
arrest every believer in Damascus" (9:13–14).
Hear the panic in his voice? Ananias did befriend
this former persecutor of Christians turned
believer and served as the instrument for Saul's
healing, filling with the Holy Spirit, and water
baptism. Ananias probably supplied him with
food and secured housing for him in Damascus
as well (verse 19).

This inaugural encouragement from believers
strengthened Saul to immediately start preaching
about Jesus in the synagogues. His early ministry
found acceptance by many Jews, but it became
apparent that some religious leaders wanted to

see him dead. Several believers helped him escape Damascus by lowering him in a basket outside the city wall. Saul fled, seeking asylum with the saints in Jerusalem. Those who help him risked their lives for his escape and greatly encouraged Saul in his newly found faith.

Barnabas, another follower of Christ, provided a major source of comfort for Saul. The Jerusalem saints were leery and afraid to embrace Saul's testimony (Acts 9:26–30). As far as they knew, he just pretended to be religious so as to throw them into prison or have them executed. The key phrase is, "But Barnabas took him and brought him to the apostles" (verse 27, NIV). Barnabas explained Saul's conversion and preaching ministry to their satisfaction (and brought great relief to Saul as well!).

Encourage others by being a Barnabas

The fourth reality: *by comforting others we often find comfort for our own struggles.* It may sound backwards, but one of the most practical things we can do to face the fear of rejection is to *encourage others by being a Barnabas.* We all need people like Barnabas in our lives but finding that person or persons can present a challenge. Sometimes we ask the wrong people.

I remember approaching a fellow minister about meeting for mutual fellowship and sharing. His response went something like this, "Sure, I'd be glad to help you out. Anytime you want to talk about something just let me know." I was looking for a fellow-struggler, not a counselor.

Several years ago I approached a few men to see if they would be interested in forming an accountability group. I had heard one of them express the desire to have some venue in which he could openly share without fear of rejection. The group would have no leader—we would be equals meeting weekly to keep one another accountable and pray for one another. Now these men are my Barnabas-types. We practice mutual encouragement, acceptance, and love.

Finding someone to encourage is often easier than finding a Barnabas-type person to help us. If we truly need a Barnabas, however, God will provide him or her in answer to our prayers.

One gloomy day I recall praying something like, "Lord, I wish someone would call today, because I'm really down." Ever felt like that? I did not want to bother anyone and wasn't sure who would understand, anyway. It's scary to feel that way. Shortly afterward, a deacon from my church phoned to see how things were going. I immediately knew God had answered my prayer—a God Sighting, if you will—and my gloom began to dissipate.

That man functioned as a Barnabas that day—and continues to be now years later. He helped me stand tall and unafraid when I felt fearful. The Lord may not provide for you in this same way, but he "gives endurance and encouragement" (Romans 15:5, NIV) and will never let us down or allow us to go very long without the support we need.

Who in your world might need a Barnabas right now? Who do you know who struggles with fear because of some dire situation? Put yourself in his or her place: "What would I appreciate receiving from someone else? What would help me?" and do that for them. Maybe send an e-mail, write a card, make a phone call, or do coffee together. Years ago I started the habit of writing cards (or e-mail) or phoning people to express my congratulations, thanks, sympathy, or prayers for them. It's just a simple way of being a Barnabas and showing acceptance and love.

Encouragement, real or imagined, makes a difference—as this frog story illustrates. A group of frogs was traveling through the woods when two of them fell into a deep pit. The other frogs looked into it and said, "You're as good as dead."

The two frogs ignored the comments and tried to jump out of the pit, but the pit was very deep. The topside frogs told them to give up and accept their fate. Finally, one of the frogs listened and gave up. He fell down, rolled over, and died. The other frog continued to jump. Once again, the crowd of frogs yelled at him to stop and just die, but he jumped even harder and finally made it out. While he rested, the other frogs said,

"Didn't you hear us?"

The frog hadn't heard them. He thought they were cheering him on the entire time![7] As Proverbs 12:25 says, "Worry weighs a person down; an encouraging word cheers a person up."

Some things to remember about being a Barnabas: (1) Go at the pace of the other person. Be sensitive to their feelings. They may not feel like opening up but may appreciate knowing of your prayers for them. (2) Back off when you sense nothing more will help. Don't allow your need to minister to take priority over their need for reassurance.

Once when hospitalized for an undiagnosed illness, I received a call from a parishioner. He proceeded to tell me his diagnosis of my problem and suggested solutions. I appreciated his thoughtfulness in phoning, even though I did not agree with his conclusions. The call went beyond helpfulness, however, when I sensed that his need for acceptance and a feeling of importance took priority. A needy person who had trouble making friends, this man called primarily to make himself feel better. A Barnabas accepts a person as is and attempts to bring cheer and well being. A Barnabas helps people loosen the grip of fear and stand tall fearful, but unafraid.

God's Word clearly tells us to encourage one another, i.e., to be a Barnabas to one another:

> Therefore encourage one another and build each other up, just as in fact you are doing. (1 Thessalonians 5:11, NIV)

> But encourage one another daily, as long as it is called Today, so that none of you may be hardened by sin's deceitfulness. (Hebrews 3:13, NIV)

> . . . let us encourage one another—and all the more as you see the Day approaching. (Hebrews 10:25b, NIV)

Remember how Sam, the rejected one, became a Barnabas to Frodo? Reaching out, even in the face of rejection, Sam brought encouragement and courage to his friend and master. *Encourage others by being a Barnabas.* Ask the Lord right now to bring people to mind who need a Barnabas touch from you. In addition to the "Unafraid Prayer," (see Chapter 2), you may also want use this prayer by Lloyd Ogilvie, former Chaplain of the U.S. Senate:

> *Secure in God's love, I will not surrender my self-worth to the opinions and judgments of others. When I am rejected, I will not retaliate; when I am hurt, I will allow God to heal me. And knowing the pain of rejection, I will seek to love those who suffer from its anguish.*[8]

Fearful, but unafraid.

[1] J. R. R. Tolkien, *The Fellowship of the Ring* (Boston: Houghton Mifflin Company, 1994) 396-397.

[2] Douglas J. Rumford, *Scared to Life* (Wheaton, IL: Victor Books, 1994) 53.

[3] John Powell, *Why Am I Afraid to Tell You Who I Am* (Niles, IL: Argus Communications, 1969) 12.

[4] John Ortberg, *If You Want to Walk on Water, You've Got to Get Out of the Boat* (Grand Rapids: Zondervan, 2001) 129-130.

[5] H. Norman Wright, *Afraid No More* (Wheaton, IL: Tyndale House Publishers, 1989) 75-76.

[6] Paul Tournier, quoted in Powell, *Why Am I Afraid* 5.

[7] <www.pastorsline.com> 4 Feb. 2003.

[8] H. N. Wright 78.

chapter four

loosening the grip of
skeletons in the closet

Skeletons in the closet, you failed to tell the truth.
Gotta monkey on your back and he's gonna bite you.
Skeletons in the closet, scaring you to death.
Gotta rope made of lies and it's wrapped around your neck.
—Frank Castro

Shocked, disappointed, and angered, Tolkien's Gandalf refuses to give his beloved former mentor any information regarding the Ring. Saruman now belongs to the darkness and is in league with the Dark Lord. No longer is he Saruman the White, but now Saruman of Many Colors. His true nature betrayed the congenial words flowing from his mouth. Gandalf soon recognized the "skeleton" of deception in Saruman's closet: "You were head of the Council, but you have unmasked yourself at last."[1]

•••

The Fibber McGee and Molly Show starring Jim and Marian Jordan of Peoria, Illinois, captured the attention of millions during the Golden Days of Radio. From 1935 to 1959 the McGees at 79 Wistful Vista in an unnamed Midwestern town brought laughter to many households. McGee, as everyone called him, had a preoccupation with saving junk and storing it in a closet.

The script for every one of the 700 broadcasts included a time when McGee wanted something from his closet. When he opened the door the audience would hear a loud crash as the fully packed closet emptied on the floor. Molly complained, but McGee always found the missing item.

What are skeletons anyway?

This is probably not the first time you've heard the term *skeletons in the closet*. In our society it refers to many things:

- One's family genealogy
- Ape-like creatures many scientists call the "missing links" to understanding how human life began.
- Old mainframe computer applications
- Names of retail shops
- Pesticides we have on hand that need to be disposed of.
- Stuff in our real closets that needs to be tossed or moved.
- General term for poor musical arrangements
- The name of several songs
- A film that bombed in 2000
- Car maintenance needs
- Glitches in computer security

GoEnglish.com defines this phrase as "things about your past which you would prefer not to tell to other people, " or, "embarrassing things which we would like to put away so other people cannot see them." We're talking about attitudes or actions we want kept secret, like:

- Family secrets
- Resume lies (GPA, degrees, titles, etc.)
- Child/Spouse Abuse
- Divorce

- Alcoholism
- Incest
- Infidelity
- Abortion
- Drugs
- Rape
- Pornography
- Bad credit rating
- Secretive business practices
- Criminal convictions
- Relationship entanglements
- Embarrassing actions

A number of sermons have been given using this phrase. Several I ran across were titled, "Skeletons in Jesus's Closet," and referred to the characters in Matthew's account of Jesus's genealogy. Most, however, dealt with sins in people's lives.

Not all people regard "skeletons" as sins necessarily, but rather, misfortunes of childhood. The mother of former President Franklin Roosevelt kept him isolated from other children for years. Oh, how he must have yearned to break free and experience more of life. He was privately tutored until age fourteen, when he left for boarding school. Roosevelt grew up with an appealing personality, but due to the lack of significant friends in his earlier years, he had difficulty all his life sharing intimate feelings. In this case the "skeleton" took the form of something that happened to him, rather than a transgression of his own, and he may have wished to keep it a family secret.

Many people live in terror that secret things in their lives will be exposed. Some long to "get it off their chest" with a trusted person. An article entitled "Dance With the Skeletons in Your Closet" on *shouldexist.org* proposes a forum called something like *SkeletonCloset.org* whereby people could tell their secrets in a safe public place anonymously or with a real or feigned names and solicit feedback. Such an approach might help, but a significant difference exists between recounting secrets to strangers, anonymously or not, than to personal acquaintances.

For our purposes we will regard skeletons in the closet as unrepented of and unconfessed sin known only to ourselves or a few people that we fear may become public knowledge. Does just the thought of the exposure of a skeleton in your life terrify you? It is a horrible fear that causes trepidation in many people. Our emphasis in this chapter concerns loosening the grip of this fear by ridding ourselves of skeletons and receiving God's gracious forgiveness. We need to stand tall and face these fears.

Nathaniel Hawthorne, in his classic work, *The Scarlet Letter,* clearly portrays this type of skeleton and the consequences of keeping the closet door shut. The story centers on an affair between a married woman, Hester, and the minister, Rev. Dimmesdale. With his child in her arms, the woman publicly admits her sin, endures insults from the townspeople, and is sentenced to prison, refusing to reveal the father's identity. On her dress she sews a red letter "A," embroidered in gold, which she must wear for life.

After seven miserable years of keeping his indiscretion secret and bearing the heavy guilt of failing to stand in public with her, the minister decides to confess. Standing on the scaffolding with Hester and their daughter Pearl, he reveals his sin. Immediately afterward, Dimmesdale dies of poor health, partly caused by the mental torment he suffered during those years. How much better for him to have stood with her those seven years than to have lived them in terror that someone would discover his secret. For those who keep skeletons in their closets, "secrecy becomes their spiritual tomb."[2]

What does the Bible say about skeletons?

The Bible clearly states that the Lord is cognizant of everything in our thoughts and on our minds: "for he knows the secrets of every heart" (Psalm 44:21b). Job 28 depicts this exhaustive knowledge using an illustration from ancient mining techniques. Mankind goes to great lengths and dangers in order to mine silver, gold, iron and copper, and precious gems, searching the darkest and deepest recesses of the earth. Torches and candles provide light, and shafts are cut where even birds do not venture. Man's efforts are like an assault on an enemy until all the secrets of the darkness are unearthed: "He searches the sources of the rivers and brings hidden things to light" (verse 11, NIV).

Scary, huh? Read on. It gets worse before it gets better. If we can discover the treasures of rocks and earth through technology, then to what greater extent can God bring *hidden things to light* in our own hearts? And when they are discovered, he will make visible those skeletons that displease him.

Miners provide artificial light to do their work. God uses the light emanating from his holy nature to search for unholiness: "You have set our iniquities before you, our secret sins in the light of your presence" (Psalm 90:8, NIV). The apostle

Paul declares that "secret thoughts will be laid bare" as people listen to the word of God (1 Corinthians 14:25), and that Christ will pass judgment on our hidden skeletons: "The day will surely come when God, by Jesus Christ, will judge everyone's secret life" (Romans 2:16). No one can hide from him or this day, for as the Lord himself asks, "Can anyone hide in secret places so that I cannot see him?" (Jeremiah 23:24, NIV). God is light, and it is light that exposes our dark closets.

Unlike Fibber McGee, who opened his closet weekly, many people don't want God or anyone else to see their skeletons and plan on keeping it that way, but the only path to peace and freedom is to expose them ourselves and *receive God's gracious forgiveness.*

Forces that set the need for forgiveness in motion

We're still in the scary part, but keep reading; it will get better soon. Before we look into all that receiving forgiveness involves, we need to understand some of the dynamics that set the need for forgiveness in motion. In my anxious experience with closeted skeletons, I have identified several forces that come into play, the first being the *decision* to create a skeleton in our closet, in other words, the moment when we say "yes" to temptation's enticement. James explains the sequence: "each one is tempted when, by his own evil desire, he is dragged away and enticed. Then, after desire has conceived, it gives birth to sin; and sin, when it is full-grown, gives birth to death" (1:14–15, NIV).

James' rich language pictures a person lured away from his current state of mind toward a baited trap, as a fish moves toward a hook. When we decide to take the bait sin occurs, followed by the desired action. The closet is where we keep all the junk we don't want company or sometimes anyone—to see. A discrepancy exists between what we do in private and in public life. When that decision and eventual act are completed, the skeleton has been fashioned in the closet. The door automatically locks and we possess the only key. Sounds evil, doesn't it? It is, and where evil exists, so does fear.

Denial enters sooner or later as another force that sets the need for forgiveness in motion. We don't like the awful pain of guilt, blame, and shame, so we protect ourselves by denying the reality of having done anything wrong—or at least minimizing its seriousness. Denial is essentially dishonest. First, we deny the truth to ourselves by justifying our actions: no harm done, not a big deal, just being human, no one's perfect, it was forced upon me, or I did nothing wrong. Second, if others become suspicious and question our actions, we deny that a problem exists at all. Evil. Fear.

Denial is a powerful force. I recall meeting with a couple considering divorce. The upset wife described her mate as irresponsible and uncaring. The impatient husband characterized his spouse as bitter and a nag. Both were right, and the husband eventually admitted to his faults. The wife, however, would not admit to her angry, nagging spirit. Looking straight at me with anger just oozing from her expression and tone of voice, she contended, "I am *not* bitter."

I've already mentioned *guilt* in relationship to denial, but it, too, is a potent dynamic. Ed Hinson defines guilt as "a self-judgment based on perceived personal misconduct."[3] A troubled conscience may produce guilt feelings such as shame, anxiety, self-condemnation, and depression.

Guilt affects people differently. When we break a law we incur guilt, whether we feel guilty or not. The terrible heaviness of guilt will either drive a person to seek forgiveness out of godly sorrow or rationalize the feeling away. Some people are so used to breaking God's laws they eventually may feel little or no guilt. A person who habitually lies, for example, has practiced falsehood so much that his or her sensitivity is numbed to sin. In this case, Paul calls such people "hypocritical liars, whose consciences have been seared as with hot irons" (1 Timothy 4:2, NIV).

Receive God's gracious forgiveness

Wouldn't it be great to boot that skeleton out of your closet and start over? Greg Laurie tells a story about a newspaper that printed the wrong person's obituary. A very upset "deceased" man showed up at the editor's desk the next day complaining about the terrible mistake. Even though the editor apologized, nothing would satisfy the distraught man, ranting and raving about his business probably suffering now and how could the editor let such an error be printed. Frustrated as well, the editor finally came up with a solution. "Look, cheer up, buddy," the editor finally said. "Tomorrow I'll put your name in the birth column, and you can have a fresh start at life."[4]

The only path to peace and freedom is to do the exposing ourselves and to *receive God's gracious forgiveness*. I know this sounds scary, but it's really the good part we've been waiting for. Fortunate is the person who feels guilt and godly sorrow over wrongdoing. This godly sorrow must lead us to a repentant attitude as Paul teaches: "your sorrow led you to repentance. . . . Godly sorrow brings repentance" (2 Corinthians 7:9–10, NIV). Repen-tance is simply a decision we make to change our thinking about sin and turn a different direction. It's a necessary step in standing tall.

On the heels of repentance is opening the door and *renouncing* the skeleton. Paul sought to convince the Corinthian church of his integrity by saying, "We have renounced secret and shameful ways" (2 Corinthians 4:2, NIV). *Renounce* means "to speak out against or disown." He spoke of false prophets who used underhanded methods to deceive the Corinthians into believing a different gospel. Paul would have nothing to do with such practices. We must have nothing more to do with that skeleton. Believe me, when you open the closet and throw away the key, things will start to change for the better.

To seek forgiveness also requires confession or agreement with God's judgment of our sin. Like David we can rest assured that "everyone who trusts in him will be freely pardoned" (Psalm 34:22b). The circumstances may require that we confess to people as well, either in private or public, in order to seek their forgiveness.

God's promises of forgiveness are plentiful. In Isaiah the Lord says, "No matter how deep the stain of your sins, I can remove it. I can make you as clean as freshly fallen snow. Even if you are stained as red as crimson, I can make you as white as wool," and, "I—yes, I alone—am the one who blots out your sins for my own sake and will never think of them again" (1:18; 43:25).

King David asked the Lord to clean out his closet, and he experienced forgiveness: "Finally, I confessed all my sins to you and stopped trying to hide them. I said to myself, 'I will confess my rebellion to the Lord.' And you forgave me! All my guilt is gone" (Psalm 32:5). Hear David's relief?

A woman caught in adultery and about to be stoned received forgiveness: "Then Jesus stood up again and said to her, 'Where are your accusers? Didn't even one of them condemn you?' 'No, Lord,' she said. And Jesus said, 'Neither do I. Go and sin no more'" (John 8:10–11). It's a wonderful feeling to get guilt off your back.

Receiving God's gracious forgiveness can be as simple as a prayer like, "Lord, forgive me, a sinner." While the attitude of our heart supercedes our words, let me suggest this simple statement of confession as a model prayer. Read it slowly and complete the sentences thoughtfully:

My Statement of Confession

I am frightened because I need to confess the sin of _____

Jesus, I am making this appeal for mercy to you because _____

My reasons for wanting to be forgiven are _____

Thank you for scriptures that encourage me, like _____

What I believe your forgiveness can do for me is _____

Right now I receive your forgiveness and express my thanks in these words _____

In the future, to be a better friend to you, I want to _____

Signed _____

Date _____

Now go back and pray these words to the Lord. After that, sign and date it as an expression of your sincerity, and trust that the Lord has cleansed your spiritual closet. Enjoy the freedom from fear forgiveness brings.

Dealing with consequences

Sometimes it's hard for us to believe we're for-given, even though God plainly says so in his Word. The consequences of sin remind us of the skeleton, like a DVD playing on continuous mode. Regret gushes in like a flash-flood and fear returns. We find ourselves rehashing the past, feeling the hurt of strained relationships, and continuing to feel guilty. We hate ourselves for what has happened and wish we had the ability to go back and change the ending, apologizing over and over to God. The intrusion of painful memories sometimes impairs our peace and free-dom.

I can identify with some of the regrets Gerald Sittser feels in his excellent book, *The Way of God as a Way of Life:*

> I regret wasting my teenage years; I was lazy and never worked at much of any-thing until I started college. I regret working such long hours when I was a pastor. I regret the fights I had with Lynda. I regret the times I have been nasty, sarcastic, and explosive with my kids. I have said words I wish I could take back, and I have committed indis-cretions I wish I could forget.[5]

If other people are involved, we may be reluctant to appear happy or normal, for fear that others will judge us as unrepentant. Or, we may know God has forgiven us but remain unforgiven by others whom we have wronged. Like prisoners in a concentration camp, we tend to allow our past skeletons to set the parameters for our lives, but we don't have to live that way.

A prisoner during World War II, psychiatrist Viktor Frankl observed how fellow inmates reacted to their circumstances. He noticed that some buckled under the extreme pressure but others chose to make the best out of a horrible situation. He concluded: "In the final analysis it becomes clear that the sort of person the prisoner became was the result of an inner decision, and not the result of camp influences alone."[6]

It's important for us to remember that *consequences* from our former skeletons differ from *forgiveness*. Nothing we can do will reverse the past. Our choices stimulate a whole set of outcomes over which we have little or no control, but they have no bearing on our forgiveness. In his unfathomable grace and mercy, our Lord says, "He has removed our rebellious acts as far away from us as the east is from the west" (Psalm 103:12, NLT), and, "If we admit our sins—make a clean breast of them—he won't let us down;

he'll be true to himself. He'll forgive our sins and purge us of all wrongdoing" (1 John 1:9, *The Message*). The key is to transfer any lingering consequences over to God to manage for our good and his honor.

We do not have to pay for our sins because Christ has already paid the price for us: "he was wounded for our transgressions, he was bruised for our guilt and iniquities" (Isaiah 53:5, AMP). Feelings of false guilt and unfounded fears are favorite tools of the devil, the enemy of our souls. When those thoughts enter our minds we need not apologize again to the Lord, rather, let us thank him for undeserved forgiveness and move on with life. If we have trouble forgiving ourselves then we haven't fully digested the worth of Christ's work on Calvary. As Erwin Lutzer comments, "If the Almighty has pronounced us clean, do we have the right to pronounce ourselves guilty?"[7]

Rather than dwell any longer on hiding skeletons in our closet, now concentrate on hiding yourself in God. If you could make only one request of God, for what would you ask? Wisdom? Security? Peace? Comfort? David chose to always live in the presence of God, delighting and meditating on him. "For," says David, "he will conceal me there when troubles come; he

will hide me in his sanctuary" (Psalm 27:5).
Listen to some of David's prayers in his own
songs as examples:

> Hide me in the shadow of your wings.
> (Psalm 17:8)

> For you are my hiding place; you pro-
> tect me from trouble. (Psalm 32:7)

> Save me from my enemies, Lord; I run
> to you to hide me. (Psalm 143:9)

In Colossians 3, Paul teaches all believers that
"Your real life is hidden with Christ in God"
(verse 3). Since this fact is true for all eternity, he
urges us to practice it in real time by focusing on
our ultimate home as we live holy lives: "Let
heaven fill your thoughts. Do not think only
about things down here on earth. . . . So put to
death the sinful, earthly things lurking within
you" (verses 2, 5). A worship song related to this
thought begins,

> *Hide me, oh Lord, in Your holiness,*
> *Every sin I now confess.*
> *Praise to You, forgiving Lord,*
> *Hide me in Your holiness.*[8]

Although offered the opportunity, Saruman
never seeks forgiveness, living out his miserable
life in fear with a closet full of skeletons.

It need not be so with us. We can loosen the grip of fear those skeletons have on us by opening the door and letting them go. We can stand tall against the fears that grip our souls by receiving the forgiveness Christ offers. I find words like these of Gerald Sittser both comforting and encouraging as I grapple from time to time with the aftermath of my skeletons:

> God can redeem our past if we let him. He redeems it by using the evil of what has happened to accomplish something good, thus transforming it so that it becomes like a vaccination. The poison ends up turning on itself, destroying the disease.[9]

[1] J. R. R. Tolkien, *The Fellowship of the Ring* (Boston: Houghton Mifflin Company, 1994) 253.

[2] Erwin Lutzer, *Putting Your Past Behind You* (Chicago: Moody Press, 1997) 17.

[3] Ed Hindson, *Overcoming Life's Toughest Problems* (Eugene, OR: Harvest House Publishers, 1999) 51.

[4] Greg Laurie, *Why Believe?* (Wheaton, IL: Tyndale House Publishers, Inc., 2002) 143.

[5] Gerald L. Sittser, *The Will of God as a Way of Life* (Grand Rapids: Zondervan Publishing House, 2000) 156.

[6] Viktor Frankl, *Man's Search for Meaning* (New York: Simon & Schuster, 1984) 87; quoted in Sittser, *Will of God,* 153.

[7] Lutzer, *Putting Your Past Behind You* 49.

[8] Steve Ragsdale, "Hide Me in Your Holiness" (Maranatha Music, 1986) <morningsong.org>.

[9] Sittser 161.

Those who look to him for help

will be radiant with joy;

no shadow of shame will darken their faces

—-Psalm 34:5

chapter five

loosening the grip of
failure & disgrace

When you take on a challenge,
it builds the core of who you are,
even if you don't perform flawlessly.
—John Ortberg

Frodo needed time alone. Should the
Fellowship stay together and go with Boromir to
fight the wars of Gondor, or should they split up
and go their own separate ways? While Frodo is
contemplating the answer, Boromir suddenly
appears, startling him.

One of the Fellowship, Boromir wants Frodo to use the Ring to help deliver Gondor from the enemy. He seems sincere at first, but soon his real intention surfaces; he wants the Ring for himself. A different personality emerges as Boromir angrily orders Frodo to hand over the Ring. The hobbit escapes his grasp when Boromir trips over a rock.

As Boromir lies upon the ground, tears come to his eyes. He cries out for Frodo to return, but Frodo has vanished. Boromir—tall and proud, the pride of Gondor, a good man—has failed the temptation of the Ring. He knows it and weeps.[1]

•••

"John, I want you to play a solo in the District Music Festival this year." I started playing trumpet in the fifth grade and continued through high school. The conductor selected me from the band to be one of three trumpeters in the high school orchestra. I played well in a group, but a solo terrified me.

When my private teacher, also the band and orchestra director, wanted me to enter a solo in the festival, fear gripped my soul. He selected a piece for me to begin memorizing and we went to work. By festival time I knew the music by heart and was playing it well. My teacher commented that if I would just play it the same way before the judges, I should qualify for the state festival.

When the dreaded day came, I sat in the room, nervously anticipating the call of my name. My hands were sweaty and I would rather have been in the dentist's chair. My accompanist started the introduction, and I lifted the trumpet to my mouth. The first thirty seconds were perfect. I could see the judges looking at me with great interest. But then, the bane of brass players befell me. My mouth went completely dry. Nothing but air came through the horn. After several attempts at wetting my lips, I gave up in disgrace. It was one of those "Please share one your most embarrassing moments in life" situations.

The judges mercifully gave me a "3" which is like getting an "C" in school. They indicated on their score sheet that I had started out wonderfully well, and if it hadn't been for my nervousness, I might have made a "1" and gone on to the State Music Festival. But the fear of failing to remember my piece and performing poorly caused me to fail anyway.

The next year my teacher wanted me to try it again; I respectfully declined, to his displeasure.

The thought terrorized me. I did, however, agree to play in a trumpet trio and received a "1." We went on to State where the trio earned a "2" (bad judges, of course). In the company of others I felt more confident. Success or failure did not depend on my performance alone.

The fear of failure often overlaps with other fears, such as rejection (Chapter 3). Both can be seen in these sample "fear of failure" scenarios:

- I'd really like to start a little business, but if it didn't it pay for itself people would consider me a failure.
- I'm facing the biggest sales opportunity of the year, but if it doesn't go through I could lose my job.
- I think marriage would be wonderful, but I'm afraid it wouldn't work out and a divorce would be awful.
- That position is just what I've been looking for, but I'm worried that my performance won't meet their standards.
- Our church needs to move forward and build, but what if we start and can't finish? What kind of testimony would that be?
- We want to start a family, but we're afraid we wouldn't be good enough parents.

- My friend needs to know the Lord and I should talk with her. But what if she gets offended and it hurts our friendship?
- I should volunteer for a certain ministry, but I'm afraid I'll do a bad job and they will never want me to help again.
- I've always wanted to study this subject, but it's been a while since I was in school. I'm afraid I won't be able to keep up and finish. Then what would I do?
- I'd really like to leave this job for something different, but what if it doesn't go well? If I don't do this I'll stagnate, but I'm really afraid to venture out.

In the film *Shipping News*, the main character, Quoyle, struggles with failure. The movie opens with him looking back in time to when his father tried teaching him to dog-paddle. As the scene plays out, Quoyle says,

> I need to imagine that I'd been given to the wrong family at birth. And that somewhere in the world my real people longed for me. From where my father stood, my failure to dog-paddle was only the first of many failures—failure to speak clearly, failure to sit up straight,

failure to make friends every time we moved to another dreary upstate town. In me, my father recognized a failed life— his own.[2]

Positive aspects of failure

Mel Farr is the most successful African-American auto dealer in America and owns the largest privately owned African-American business. What drives Mel Farr? "My motivation is the fear of failure."[3]

A denominational leader once said, "As I travel and talk to our pastors I have come to the conclusion that their number-one motivation in ministry is the fear of failure."[4]

Michael Jordan, has said, "I've failed over and over and over again in my life, and that is why I succeed," and "I can accept failure, but I can't accept not trying."[5]

"Always do what you are afraid to do," voiced Ralph Waldo Emerson.[6]

Charlie Brown knew failure as well: "Sometimes I lie awake at night, and I ask, 'Where have I gone wrong?' Then a voice says to me, 'This is going to take more than one night.'"[7]

The inspectors had come and gone. They left their report with the Group Commander— one of two possible grades: Pass or Fail. Guess what? My department failed the preliminary examination. My heart must have beat faster and I couldn't get the fear of failing the final exam off my mind. My status as Personnel Officer for an Army Artillery Group would suddenly become up for grabs if we didn't pass the "real" inspection in two weeks. I could just imagine them reassigning me to field duty, or worse, sending me back to Vietnam. I had relied on the vast experience and skill of the personnel sergeant to get us through; however, he planned to retire soon and probably didn't care whether we passed or failed. Besides, some of the "seasoned" sergeants just loved seeing young lieutenants squirm.

I hated the next two weeks, during which the schedule and grind was horrible, and the Lieutenant Colonel and Major breathed down my neck more than once daily. The fear of failure was ever-present on my mind. The only time I experienced any peace was when I took a latrine break! My staff and I (including that Master Sergeant) worked hard. I read the inspector's findings, assigned people to correct the deficiencies, and personally reviewed all the work. When D-Day came, we passed with flying colors. Both my superiors and I felt great relief (so did the Master Sergeant!). Oh yes, I kept my position and was even commended for a job well done.

The fear of failure does have a positive side. That personnel shop was better organized than ever and my men felt good about their accomplishment. I prayed many times for Jesus to show me what to do next during those weeks and I also learned that he does indeed answer prayer and that failure doesn't have to repeat itself.

Carol Kent, author of *Tame Your Fears,* sees failure as having a positive contribution in her life: "It leads me to explore the depth of my disappointment, which has the potential of bringing me to a place of personal and spiritual growth. . . . I can allow failure to launch me in a different direction."[8] John Ortberg agrees: "When I allow myself to experience the pain of failure, it can drive me to make the changes that will lead to new learning."[9]

In an interesting book, *Seizing Your Divine Moment,* Erwin McManus writes:

> We fail to see divine moments when all we see is danger and the risk of failure. . . . You cannot fail without risk-

ing. . . . Failure is a part of God's environment for shaping our character. I figured out a long time ago that God wasn't interested in our having a perfect season. . . . And allowing us to fail is not a punishment from God, but a part of God's process for shaping who we are.[10]

Unbelief does a number on us

In Psalm 34:5 the Lord gives us a word of advice and a promise. The guidance he indirectly gives is to take our fear of failure to him, to "look to him for help." That's not hard to do, but it's amazing how many times we neglect simply talking it over with the Lord. Lloyd Ogilvie writes, "Fear is only a hairbreadth away from faith. When we surrender our fear, telling God how we feel, we allow faith to force out fear. Tell God, 'I'm afraid.'"[11]

The tough part is to believe his word of assurance. Here he says if we bring our fears to him joy will light up our face in place of shame: "Those who look to him for help will be radiant with joy; no shadow of shame will darken their faces." Believing this promise works, whether we have already failed at something or are currently fearful of failure. God is able to give joy in anticipation of or in the midst of failure. Ortberg writes, "Failure in our day often carries with it shame—the shame not just of having experienced failure, but of being a failure."[12]

Both joy and terror characterized the Hebrews' exodus from Egypt. Camped at Pi Hahiroth, the new nation found itself trapped against the Red Sea by six hundred Egyptian soldiers. The scripture says, "They were terrified and cried out to the Lord" (Exodus 14:10, NIV). Picture it—a million or so unarmed Israelite men, women, and children against Pharaoh's best warriors. In a panic they prayed for deliverance and then began criticizing Moses for leading them away from their homes (Exodus 14:10–12). Moses replied,

> "Do not be afraid. Stand firm and you will see the deliverance the Lord will bring you today. The Egyptians you see today you will never see again. The Lord will fight for you; you need only to be still." Then the Lord said to Moses, "Why are you crying out to me? Tell the Israelites to move on." (Exodus 14:13–15, NIV)

Note the all too familiar pattern:

1. The people cry out in fear (verse 10). People usually look to God in fearful situations.

2. They place blame on Moses, not God (verses 11–12). Moses represents God. If we can't find someone to blame we sometimes blame God for our troubles. All we can see is catastrophic failure ahead.

3. Moses has the advantage of knowing the end result (verses 1–4). He tells them not to fear and to stand firm, hold on, and be still (verses 13–14). Watch and see what the Lord is going to do. Often we need a calming down period before faith can force out fear and we can "see" clearly again.

4. After Moses gets the people somewhat under control, the Lord tells them to stop praying and get going (verse 15). God gives us proactive instructions and guidance with which to face our fears. Moses raises his staff, stretches out his hand, waits for the ground to dry, and moves out. God never fails to guide us, but we fail to listen and believe him. Fear shrivels up when we move forward in faith. In *Feel the Fear and Do It Anyway*, Susan Jeffers comments, "The only way to get rid of the fear of doing

something is to go out and do it."[13]

The story of the twelve spies returning from Canaan demonstrates the powerful grip of fear (Numbers 13—14). Ten of the twelve spies foresee disaster if Israel tries to conquer the land. Their argument includes these points:

> "But the people who live there are powerful."
>
> "The cities are fortified and very large."
>
> "We even saw descendants of Anak" (known for their gigantic proportions).
>
> "We can't attack those people; they are stronger than we are."
>
> "The land we explored devours those living in it."
>
> "All the people we saw there are of great size."
>
> "We seemed like grasshoppers in our own eyes, and we looked the same to them." (NIV)

Picking up on this last statement, Erwin Lutzer alleges that the Israelites had a "Grasshopper Complex": "We adopt the Grasshopper Complex whenever we turn away from a God-given challenge for fear that we lack resources to tackle it, or when we try to avoid facing a problem that is hindering our spiritual progress."[14]

Once again the people cry out in fear. Once again they blame Moses. Once again Moses tells them, "Do not be afraid" (14:9, NIV). Once again the Lord gives instructions but this time the people rebel. But fear wins out, and Israel continues their nomadic lifestyle for forty more unnecessary years. Their hesitation of unbelief only increased their anxiety.

Do you fear failure in some area of your life? Has the Lord brought an area of fear to your mind as you have been reading? Doing nothing assures failure. As Norm Wright maintains, "When we allow the fear of failure to dominate us, we are demanding a guaranteed outcome in the situation. But a guaranteed outcome takes away the opportunity to live by faith and trust God for the outcome."[15] Let's resolve to stand tall against the fears that grip our soul.

Perform one outrageously courageous act

"John, the mail's here. There's something from school," my mom announced. I had just finished my third semester in college and was anxious to get the grade report. I was not prepared for the results of one class. You've guessed it, haven't you? A big, fat "F" in a four-hour course. Devastated, I just could not believe it. In thirteen and a half years of school I had never failed a course (and haven't since). Fearful of facing my parents, I kept the grade report and fled to my room. Later, I reluctantly shared the painful results with them. Oddly enough, in the midst of failure, it was a memorable moment where I sensed my parent's love and support.

I called the professor. Surely he was mistaken. Hadn't I passed all the tests during the semester? I received no sympathy. He based my "F" (it still hurts to say that) mainly on failing the final exam, a multiple choice test where you received one point for every right answer, zero points for no answer, and minus two points for a wrong answer. All the scores were low, but the curve put me lower than most.

I knew he'd been watching me all semester. I sat haplessly in the front row of a class of about one hundred students—and at 7:30 AM four days a week! I'm sure he saw me nod off frequently. I didn't participate much because I found the subject and textbook pretty dull. Thus, no breaks would come my way from him.

Not only did I feel like a failure, but I had literally failed—and that felt terrible. Fearful, but unafraid, I determined to do something totally unconventional the next semester, because I never wanted to experience that again. Rather than follow the plan of required classes outlined for my course of study I signed up for classes that really interested me: you know, the ones you always wanted to take but couldn't fit in your required course of study. Also, I limited my course work to fourteen hours to ease some of the pressure.

I set my goal to get my grades back up and enjoy doing it. The plan worked—my GPA rose considerably. It cost an extra semester in college to get the required hours for graduation, but it was worth it. I resolved never, ever to fail a class again (and to avoid 7:30 AM classes, too)!

How about you? What outrageously coura-geous act could you perform to demonstrate courage during this Adventure and put fear in its proper place? Sound crazy? We're talking about doing something foreign to your usual way of thinking. Perhaps it's something you've wanted to do, but fear has held you back. Here are some ideas to stimulate your creativity:

- Try out for the praise band or choir.
- Look into a part-time job.
- Help serve meals to street folks or tutor kids.
- Train to be a crisis pregnancy counselor.

- Offer to teach or help in a class at church.
- Attend a local city council meeting and speak out on a current issue.
- Sponsor a Backyard Bible Club in the summer.
- Start an evangelistic Bible study in your neighborhood or health club.
- Welcome the next new neighbor on your block with some goodies.
- Sign up for a mission work team trip.
- Write an article and submit it to magazines.
- Join a small group.
- Volunteer in a hospital or as an election judge.

Ask the Lord what he wants you to do and for the courage to carry it through. You'll want to plan well and set a date to start. Then, as the Lord said to Moses and Israel, "Move on" (Exodus 14:15, NIV)—do it ! Let me say at this point that what we do with the current fear will determine how we face that fear the next time. If we confront it courageously we are more apt to do likewise the next time. If we shy away from it, we'll still be fearful when it or a similar fear comes around again.

I'll never forget the day I learned to downhill ski. I spent the morning on the bunny hill taking a lesson. I learned fast and felt pretty smug about my ability until my friends who already skied well said, "After lunch you're going with us up to the top." My mind filled with fear not only of failure but also embarrassment, injury, and even death!

So up we went, beyond the treeline. My first fear was of stumbling off the chair lift at the top. That realized, I picked myself up and followed my friends to the nearest run. It wasn't a bunny slope! The angle of descent appeared to be about 45 degrees—no way could I ski down this hill, but turning back wasn't an option. It was like the trumpet solo routine repeating itself! So, down (literally) I went—sometimes skiing, most of the time rolling down the hill until I reached a flatter area. From there on I took the nearest "green" trail and had a ball.

Did I ever go back to the top? I sure did. The second attempt went better and the rest is history. Ortberg's words are so true:

> When you take on a challenge, it builds the core of who you are, even if you don't perform flawlessly. . . . If you live in fear, you will never experience the potential that God has placed in you. . . . Growth always involves risk, and risk always involves fear.[16]

Guilt-ridden from his failure with Frodo and the Ring, Boromir single-handedly kills twenty Orcs in one last outrageously courageous act to save Merry and Pippin. Later, Aragorn finds him sitting underneath a tree with his sword, wounded by several Orc arrows. Boromir confesses his failure with Frodo and describes his attempt to fight off the Orcs. Just before Boromir dies, Aragorn assures him, "'No!' . . . taking his hand and kissing his brow. 'You have conquered.'"[17]

One of the top three most requested quotes by Theodore Roosevelt keeps bumping into me as I wade through literature on failure. Roosevelt made this statement in 1910 at the Sorbonne, Paris. I cite part of it now for my own sake as much as for yours, as a good reminder:

> The credit belongs to the man who is actually in the arena . . . who errs and comes up short again and again . . . who, at the best, knows, in the end, the triumph of high achievement, and who, at the worst, if he fails, at least he fails while daring greatly, so that his place shall never be with those cold and timid souls who knew neither victory nor defeat.[18]

[1] J. R. R. Tolkien, *The Fellowship of the Ring* (Boston: Houghton Mifflin Company, 1994) 390.

2   *Shipping News,* dir. Lasse Hallström, DVD, Buena Vista Home Entertainment, 2002.

3   John Pepper, *Detroit Daily News,* August 17, 1997; quoted in Neil T. Anderson and Rich Miller, *Freedom from Fear* (Eugene, OR: Harvest House Publishers, 1999) 143–144.

4   Neil Anderson and Rich Miller, *Freedom from Fear* (Eugene, OR: Harvest House Publishers, 1999), 144.

5   *House of Quotes Page* <www.houseofquotes.com>.

6   Ibid.

7   <pastors.com>.

8   Carol Kent, *Tame Your Fears* (Colorado Springs, CO: NavPress, 2003) 204.

9   John Ortberg, *If You Want to Walk on Water, You've Got to Get Out of the Boat* (Grand Rapids: Zondervan, 2001) 144.

10 Erwin Raphael McManus, *Seizing Your Divine Moment* (Nashville: Thomas Nelson Publishers, 2002) 139, 141.

11 Lloyd John Ogilvie, *Lord of the Impossible* (Nashville: Abingdon, 1984) 70; quoted in Wright, *Afraid No More* 107.

12 Ortberg 141.

13 Susan Jeffers, *Feel the Fear and Do It Anyway* (New York: Fawcett Columbine, 1987) 4; quoted in Neil T. Anderson and Rich Miller *Freedom from Fear* (Eugene, OR: Harvest House Publishers, 2000) 157.

14 Erwin Lutzer, *Conquering the Fear of Failure* (Ann Arbor, MI: Vine Books, 2002) 15.

15 H. N. Wright 110.

16 Ortberg 125, 127.

17 J. R. R. Tolkien, *The Two Towers* (Boston: Houghton Mifflin Company, 1994) 403–404.

18 Theodore Roosevelt, "Citizenship in a Republic," Speech at the Sorbonne, Paris, 23 April 1910; cited on <www.theodoreroosevelt.org>.

Even when I walk through the dark valley of death,

I will not be afraid, for you are close beside me. . . .

I cried out to the Lord in my suffering,

and he heard me.

He set me free from all my fears.

—Psalm 23:4; 34:6

chapter six

loosening the grip of
disease & death

The weariest and most loathed worldly life that age,
ache, penury, and imprisonment can lay on nature,
is a paradise to what we fear of death.
—William Shakespeare, *Measure for Measure*

Tolkien's little band faces many terrifying moments on its adventure in Middle Earth, none so frightening, for Gandalf at least, as when threatened by the hideous Balrog in the mines of Moria.

Knowing only he could save his comrades from death, Gandalf stands bravely between them and the fiery beast. With staff in hand, he forbids the Balrog from crossing the bridge toward them. When the creature approaches anyway, Gandalf lifts his staff and strikes the bridge, breaking it in half and sending the Balrog to its death.

But, as it falls, the beast's whip-like tail wraps around Gandalf's knees, pulling him toward the edge. Unable to hold on to the crumbling rock, he, too, falls into the abyss. Gandalf stands tall against the fear of death and by doing so rescues eight members of the Fellowship.[1] He is fearful, but unafraid.

•••

One day I awoke with what felt like something in my eye. I tried the usual procedures for cleansing but nothing worked. Later in the day I drove to a convenient care facility. The doctor couldn't find anything wrong and assessed it as some kind of irritation (I knew that!). He gave me a patch to wear for two days—the drive home with one eye was a precarious experience!

I couldn't see to work so I stayed home for those two days but nothing changed, so we scheduled an appointment with an opthamologist. He diagnosed my problem as a viral infection and put me on some medications. However, the aggravating, scratchy irritation increased and the eye drained continually. I kept seeing the doctor but he said to give the medicine time and take ibuprofen if needed.

Eventually, I started breaking out around the eye and left side of my forehead. My wife rushed me to the doctor and he finally got the diagnosis right: Shingles. He prescribed a different medicine, but later at home it got worse, and I ended up in the hospital for several days with severe pain and nausea.

I began to worry that this disease might harm my vision. The nausea and pain lessened, but the eye continued to drain and hurt. Exposure to normal or bright light was unbearable, so I could not drive, work, read, watch television, have curtains open or have bright lights on. After a month of this misery, we sought a second opinion and stayed with the new physician. Eventually, he found and prescribed a different medicine and things begin to clear up. The cornea, however, was permanently scarred.

I hadn't been afraid of getting Shingles, because who would have thought? But now, I occasionally get fearful that those little viruses might wake up and counter-attack, like Orcs seeking revenge. Like many people, I also have some apprehension about cancer cells possibly growing inside somewhere, or how thick the cholesterol is coating my arteries, or to what extent arthritis may limit my activity. Or what about AIDS? As my wife lay sick in the hospital recently receiving blood, I was thankful for the person who gave that blood but wondered, even though blood is screened now, what if any potential problems arise?

People fear well-known diseases like cancer in all its varieties, heart attacks, Parkinson's, and Alzheimer's, and even less common illnesses such as Multiple Sclerosis, Lupus, Bells Palsey, Gillian Beres, or the West Nile or other super-viruses. Most of us know people who have suffered from these or similar conditions. Just knowing about their suffering tends to make us fearful that we may join their ranks one day, especially if they are family members.

Sometimes we'll try anything to avoid disease. CNN reported that several years ago Montana resident Stan Jones, 63, was so afraid that Y2K might make antibiotics scarce that he made his own medicine. Hearing that colloidal silver supplements could protect you from disease, he electrically charged two silver wires in a glass of water and drank it daily. Before long his skin began to turn blue—a permanent condition called argvria. The news report went on to mention that Jones lost his campaign for election to the U. S. Senate from the Libertarian party—"Talk about a red, white and BLUE candidate."[2]

Disease means suffering and may lead to death—perhaps the ultimate fear. We're reminded of death daily when an ambulance or funeral procession drives by, when we see death portrayed on many television programs and films, or when we read the obituaries in the paper. The other day while picking up a prescription I saw a product facing me on the pharmacy counter. It was a box of pills to take in case of a nuclear attack to protect you from the affects of radiation.

The fear of death can drive people to other extremes, like Sarah Winchester, wife of the famous rifle manufacturer. After his death from influenza, she sought the guidance of a medium who told her that as long as she kept building on a house she need never fear death. She immediately purchased a seventeen-room mansion and began expanding it. For years she supervised ongoing construction projects. By the time she died, the mansion had 150 rooms, 13 bathrooms, 2000 doors, 47 fireplaces, and 10,000 windows. A tourist attraction today in San Jose, California, it still stands as a monument to the fear of death.[3]

Fairy tale author Hans Christian Andersen feared being buried alive. He often carried a note or left it by his bedside informing people that he may only "seem dead." He died of cancer at age 70 after a lifetime of fear.[4]

Reasons we may fear disease

Why do we fear disease and bodily trauma? (1) *We don't want to suffer.* Whether it's the twenty-four hour flu or a major disease—we don't welcome pain or suffering. Most of us would agree that one of the ingredients of "life at its best" would be a 100% healthy body.

(2) *We don't want to lose our dignity and lifestyle.* Depending on the severity of illness, we may suffer embarrassing loss of control over caring for ourselves and our bodily function. It may mean long-term hospital and/or home care, change in lifestyle, permanent disability, disfigurement, or loss or diminishment of mental abilities. Family or friends may avoid us and drop out of our lives. Permanent nursing home care means separation from our homes and family.

I knew a man who contracted an illness which left him without memory of his occupational skills. He'd been a skilled technician for years but could not remember enough to keep his job. In

addition, the disease slightly changed his personality so that he became less patient and even
angry at times. His loss was overwhelmingly frus-
trating to him and his family.

Reasons we may fear death

Some people have no apparent fear of dying. I
stood beside the bedside of a godly woman in a
nursing home. Her husband finally admitted he
could no longer care for this good woman. What
a positive couple they were—always cheerful and
so supportive of the church. Against her wishes,
the decision was made for her to live in a nearby
nursing home. The day she arrived, she stopped
speaking.

Coma-like, she did not respond to anything I
said. Then I mustered up some courage and said
to her, "I know you can hear me and what you're
doing. You don't want to be here, do you, and
you're just waiting to be with the Lord?" No
response—except, I'm sure I saw a twinkle in her
eye and a slight smile-like curve to her mouth. It
wasn't many days until she got her wish. And it
wasn't many months until her husband joined
her in death. She did not fear death—she wel-
comed it.

Others cover fear over with pleasure-seeking
thereby delaying thoughts of the inevitable. Some

believe all life ends with death and nothing lies ahead. A CBS *60 Minutes II* program on assisted suicide (February 2003) featured an 81-year-old retired German mechanical engineer suffering from Parkinson's Disease. Ernst Aschmoneit had elected to terminate his life with the help of a Swiss agency. Dignitas is an alternative assisted suicide group that has as its purpose helping people die with dignity. The procedure is legal as long as no one profits, the patient administers the drug him- or herself, an agency representative is present, and they have determined to their satisfaction that the person has made a rational choice.

Correspondent Lara Logan interviewed Aschmoneit a few minutes before he drank the toxic barbiturate. He looked and sounded calm, shared that his life had been good and that he did not want to live any longer with his disease. For him, death meant release from pain and suffering and led to nothingness. He would simply be gone forever.

King David feared death because his enemies sought to kill him: "My heart is in anguish. The terror of death overpowers me. Fear and trembling overwhelm me. I can't stop shaking" (Psalm 55:4–5). Most of us, however, don't have "hit men" after us. Many fear death because,

(1) *we don't want to go through the process of dying.* This process may include some of the implications mentioned above in the first reason we fear disease. Until this point, we have always recovered. Not so with death from which none of us will recuperate.

(2) *We don't want to lose life because that's all we know.* We don't know what it's like on the other side. Judgment? Nothing? Heaven? Hell? Even if life isn't all we bargained for, most of us hold on as long as we can. As Brian Stiller explains,

> Though we have snippets of stories of those who say they have ventured across the divide and returned, and even though we may have a deep-rooted belief in what life will be like, death is an enormous shift of all we've known.[5]

(3) *We also don't want to lose relationships, especially with God.* We don't want to die alone, without loved ones. We may be fearful of facing God.

(4) *We may have a genuine fear of leaving loved ones to fend for themselves.* A friend told me that she was only four years old when her mother died. When her first child reached four, she became very fearful of dying and leaving her chil-

dren without a mother. She questioned God's goodness and searched the scriptures for theological answers. Her fear returned with the second child's fourth birthday, but this time her questioning was more personal and less theological. She eventually was able to give her children over to God and his love.

Stiller asks a penetrating question: "So how do I face that, regardless of my age or physical well-being, I'm dying? Do I see it, as did Carl Jung, as the fulfillment of life's meaning? Or as Jean Paul Sartre suggested, the ultimate absurdity?"[6] Many people assume life will last until some time in older age. Some block out the thought of death with busyness, or just train themselves to switch off those thoughts to something more positive.

Ray and Nancy Kane, in *From Fear to Love,* suggest that some people keep death out of their consciousness by immersing themselves in causes of lasting worth. They conclude, however, that "While many of these activities may help humanity for the greater good, they never take away our terror of being unable to control our own destinies."[7]

A better way

A better way to face the fear, sometimes terror, of disease and death is to contemplate the meaning of life. When we do, we discover that *(1) suffering is part of being human.* Douglas Rumford is right on when he says: "We presume that sickness is abnormal, something we should never have to cope with. . . . We are beginning to demand cures as if they were among our inalienable rights, instead of receiving them as gifts."[8]

James 4:13–16 warns us of attempting to manage our brief lives apart from the will of God. "How do you know what will happen tomorrow?" the Lord asks us. He says we're just going our own independent way unless we can say with James, "If the Lord wants us to, we will live and do this or that."

Stiller adds, "For dying is really about living. Facing life is the core challenge."[9] When we stand tall against life and its fears, we move forward, and this becomes the second reality we discover when we contemplate life: *(2) Suffering produces growth.* The apostle Paul wrote about this growth: "We also rejoice in our sufferings, because we know that suffering produces perseverance; perseverance, character; and character, hope" (Romans 5:3–4, NIV). We become more like Jesus in his humanity and compassion. Now that I know the pain of shingles in my eye, I feel more compassionate toward those likewise afflicted.

A third reality we discover is that eventually all suffering will cease: *(3) Death means the end of suffering and sin.* The prophet Isaiah foretold the death experience: "He will swallow up death forever. The Sovereign Lord will wipe away the tears from all faces; he will remove the disgrace of his people from all the earth" (Isaiah 25:8, NIV). Paul says death will be "swallowed up in victory" (1 Corinthians 15:54). It is permanent, irreversible, and final. Life is "drunk down" along with its sorrows, failures, and afflictions.

The fourth reality: *(4) Death means we're home.* Whether I'm gone for several weeks or a day, it's always good to be home again. God lovingly carries home his believing children in Christ: "Precious in the sight of the Lord is the death of his saints" (Psalm 116:15, NIV).

In his work on *Holy Dying,* Jeremy Taylor urges us to live without complaining about the many troubles we face and to consider death as a merciful end to suffering. "For," he writes, "a man at least gets this by death, that his calamities are not immortal."[10]

King David is a good example of being fearful but unafraid. If he could be with us today and ease our fears about disease and death he would share his own testimony:

I cried out to the Lord in my suffering, and he heard me. He set me free from all my fears.

Even when I walk through the dark valley of death, I will not be afraid, for you are close beside me. (Psalm 34:6; 23:4)

Asaph, another psalmist, exhorts us with similar words: Your health may fail, and your spirit may grow weak, but God remains the strength of your heart; he is yours forever (Psalm 73:26, my paraphrase).

Muslim guerillas murdered New Tribes missionary Martin Burnham in May 2001, when the Philippine military raided the camp. Both Martin and his wife, Gracia, had thought much about the possibility of death over their 376-day captivity and prepared themselves for whatever the Lord wanted.

Just minutes before three bullets fatally wounded Martin and another went through Gracia's leg, Martin said: "We may not leave this jungle alive, but we can leave this world serving the Lord 'with gladness'; we can 'come before his presence with singing'" (Psalm 100:2, KJV). Later, Gracia wrote, "Now that I've come home to focus on my children for the next few years, I am determined to keep serving the Lord 'with gladness,' as Martin emphasized that last rainy afternoon we spent together."[11]

Write your own epitaph or eulogy

What's a practical way to loosen the grip of these fears? How about writing your own epitaph or eulogy? An epitaph is a brief statement that summarizes or "epitomizes" someone who has died; it's found on a tombstone or grave marker. It captures the essence of a person's life. A eulogy is a public speech praising the virtues and achievements of a deceased person. Look at this epitaph in Waynesville, North Carolina:

> *Effie Jean Robinson*
> *1897-1922*
> *Come blooming youths, as you pass by,*
> *And on these lines do cast an eye.*
> *As you are now, so once was I;*
> *As I am now, so must you be;*
> *Prepare for death and follow me.*

Underneath, someone has added:

> *To follow you*
> *I am not content,*
> *How do I know*
> *Which way you went.*[12]

Compare that to one from Halifax, Nova Scotia, Fairview Lawn Cemetary:

*Sacred
to the memory of
Everett Edward Elliot
of the heroic crew S.S. "Titanic"
died on duty April 15, 1912
Age 24 years
Each man stood at his post
while all the weaker ones went by,
and showed once more to all the world
how Englishmen should die.*[14]

Some people have interesting descriptions, like Ralph Waldo Emerson's tombstone in Sleepy Hollow Cemetery, Concord, Massachusetts:

*The passive master lent his hand,
To the vast Soul which o'er him planned.*[15]

The purpose of this exercise is to loosen the grip of fear of disease and death through the process of analyzing what kind of person we want our disease or even death to forge out of the melting pot of suffering. How do we want people to remember us? Do we want to be a complaining person, always bewailing our physical misfortunes? I really enjoy being around those people, don't you?! Through the years I've learned so much from visiting ill folks. I've seen the kind just described, but a select few exemplified a wonderful spirit in suffering.

One lady I knew often had some sort of physical problem, but always had a cheery smile, even when lying on a hospital bed in severe pain. I do not remember ever hearing her complain. She always gave praise to her Lord for what he enabled her to do, seldom dwelling on her limitations. Usually, she would quickly turn the conversation over to how I or someone else was getting along. Always pleasant to call upon, she exemplified godly suffering.

What you just read was a brief eulogy. A fitting epitaph for her might be:

> *She loved her Lord.*
> *She loved her family.*
> *She suffered greatly—*
> *But never complained—*
> *Only that she could not do more*
> *for her Lord, whom she manifested*
> *in her pain.*

When I think about death, it seems I am more fearful of the process than the actual moment of dying, because of my belief in a resurrected Christ, who lived and died to conquer death for those who trust him. If we have a true Christian understanding of death, we can look forward to spending eternity with Christ. When those last hours come for us, may our attitudes harmonize with that of the sister of Donald Grey Barnhouse, pastor for thirty-three years of Tenth Presbyterian Church in Philadelphia. When the time was near she spoke about people coming to visit and her view of death,

> They know I am going to die, and I know it, but they are afraid to speak about it. But death is not fearful. . . . Life is like living in a darkened room. You get glimpses of a sunlit garden outside, but you are living in the shadow. Death is the door that takes you out of the shadowy room of life into the sunlit presence of the Lord Jesus Christ. I am so glad to have come to that door.[17]

[1] J. R. R. Tolkien, *The Fellowship of the Ring* (Boston: Houghton Mifflin Company, 1994) 322.

[2] CNN, 2 October 2002.

[3] Vernon Grounds, *Our Daily Bread.*

[4] M.R. DeHaan II, *Our Daily Bread.*

[5] Brian C. Stiller, *What Happens When I Die?* (Colorado Springs: Pinion Press, 2001) 33.

[6] Stiller 35.

[7] Ray and Nancy Kane, *From Fear to Love* (Chicago: Moody Press, 2002) 110.

8   Douglas J. Rumford, *Scared to Life* (Wheaton, IL: Victor Books, 1994) 109.

9   Stiller 37.

10 Jeremy Taylor, *The Rule and Exercises of Holy Living and the Rule and Exercises of Holy Dying* (Wilton, CN: Morehouse-Barlow Co., 1981) 52; quoted in Rumford, *Scared* 116.

11 Gracia Burnham, *In The Presence of My Enemies* (Wheaton, IL: Tyndale House Publishers, 2003) 262, 306.

12 <webpanda.com/ponder/epitaphs.htm>.

13 Ibid.

14 <alsirat.com/epitaphs/index.html>.

15 Ibid.

16 Ibid.

17 Donald Barnhouse, *Romans, Vol. III* (Grand Rapids: Wm. B. Eerdmans Publishing, 1982) 213.

The righteous face many troubles,
but the Lord rescues them
from each and every one.
—Psalm 34:19

chapter seven

loosening the grip of
paralyzing what-ifs

What if this happens? What if that happens?
A great deal of time and tremendous energy are consumed
worrying about what may never actually transpire.
—Greg Laurie

When she stopped receiving daily letters from Vietnam the lieutenant's wife feared something dreadful had happened. Unbeknown to her, something quite unexpected had indeed taken place.

They married in February, took a long honeymoon, and left their hearts in San Francisco as the husband departed for "Nam" in April. They immediately began counting down from 180 the days until they could meet for R&R in Hawaii, or perhaps Australia, halfway through the one-year tour. She settled in her nursing job in Minnesota and he worked at getting used to life in a strange new country at war.

A worrisome week or so after the letters stopped arriving, the phone rang. It was the Red Cross. Can you imagine the apprehension she must have felt? Her husband had been wounded over a week ago. He had spent a week in a DaNang intensive care unit and then been transferred to an Army hospital in Japan. During that first week in DaNang, the Red Cross said they would notify his wife, but it didn't happen. Either an error took place or they wanted to see if he would make it first.

The lieutenant's wife immediately tried phoning the hospital. After numerous delays, she finally got through at the same time her husband was in physical therapy. He told her about the booby trap that had exploded in front of him and the resulting wounds. The fact that he was in physical therapy made her nervous.

> *What if his wounds are life threatening?*
> *What if he's lost a limb or more?*

What if he's not telling me the truth?
What if they don't give him proper treat-
   ment?
What if they send him back to Vietnam?
What if I won't recognize him?

She suspected (she later confessed) that he kept the seriousness of the injuries from her. So she had to live with these fears a few more weeks until finally they reunited at a Denver Army hospital.

The "not knowing" part made the situation so difficult for my wife in this story; yet, I know she daily committed this situation to God and found strength in his Word in order to cope with such a difficult situation to face. Truly, she must have suffered more from anxiety than I did from pain. To be fair, sometimes situations like this force us to pray and wait—it's out of our hands and in God's.

A fearful time for me occurred during Army Officer Candidate School. Part of the training involved learning how to rappel. As I waited nervously in line atop a 200-foot cliff, my mind conjured up all kinds of scenarios beginning with "what if?" *What if I don't get hooked up right? What if the rope breaks? What if the person below doesn't hold onto the rope? What if I stumble and fall before they connect me? What if I chicken out? What if I don't do good enough to pass?*

"Candidate White!" *Oh, no, it's finally my turn,* I thought. They hitched me up, gave some quick instructions to hold the rope a certain way, lean back, take a step backward, loosen my grip little by little on the rope, and keep close to the cliff. "Don't jump or you'll swing back and bump against the rock," they said. That was reassuring! No way was I going to jump anywhere, except perhaps forward.

Before I could ask for clarification they nudged me off the cliff. "Oh, Lord, here we go." I caught on well enough to start down the mountain. After a few seconds I began thinking, "This is really fun!" and pushed myself away from the cliff to speed up my descent. Fear and worry turned almost instantaneously into delight. When my feet touched ground, I wanted to go back up and do it again!

Outward Bound has a motto: "If you can't get out of it, get into it." At the top I could have said, "No way, Sir, I'm not doing this." As a consequence I would have been dismissed from the program after nearly six months of training. Since my goal was to finish, that wasn't an option. I find it interesting that the key to sliding down the cliff and facing my fear involved "loosening my grip" on the rope and trusting the men and equipment.

What is worry?

It's true that we could apply "what if" to every fear thus covered in this book, but the particular emphasis in this chapter will concern unlearning fearful thought patterns. We'll choose "worry" as our operative word, defined as "a conscious choice people make to deal with problems in an ineffective way that implies the absence of a loving God."

We usually lump fear, worry, and anxiety together as synonyms, for they all express troubled states of mind. Depending on the dictionary you are using, to fear is to be anxious, to be anxious is to worry, to worry is to be anxious or fearful, and so on. "Anxious" is derived from the Latin *angere,* which means to torment or choke. "Worry," from Old English *wyrgan,* also signifies to choke or strangle, or to tear at the throat with the teeth. Both describe the suffocating effect fear can have on us. We could easily substitute "worried" or "anxious" for "afraid" in this statement: "I'm afraid something terrible has happened to Bill—he's not usually this late."

H. Norman Wright calls fear and worry first cousins but maintains that worry and anxiety have an even closer alliance.[1] He agrees they are often synonymous but points out that anxiety can have a positive side. Positive anxiety helps a musician, actor, or athlete perform better. It can stimulate a businessperson to make a better presentation. The good side of anxiety arouses creativity, interest, and ambition, as well as forewarning us of potential hazardous circumstances.

Worry concerns itself with the unknown future and is non-productive and even destructive by nature. One of the Mayo brothers commented, "You can worry yourself to death but you cannot worry yourself to a longer life."[2]

An Arab chief tells about a spy captured and sentenced to death by a firing squad. The general in charge had a unique custom of giving criminals the choice of whether to be shot or to choose whatever may lie behind a door, called "the big, black door."

Given this choice, the spy deliberated a long time. You can almost hear him thinking, "What if I take that door—will it be a worse form of death? Will it be torture? What if it might mean freedom—is it worth the risk?" The spy chose to face the firing squad.

After the execution, the general commented to his aide, "They always prefer the known to the unknown. People fear what they don't know."

"What lies beyond the big door?" asked the aide.

"Freedom," replied the general. "I've known only a few brave enough to take that door."[3]

It's true. The unknown presents a huge problem to the average person and causes us to worry about everything. For example, what if:

- I lose my health?
- I lose my money?
- I'm laid off work?
- I have a car accident?
- I lose a limb?
- I get passed over for promotion?
- I lose a loved one?
- My loved ones are threatened?
- I lose my sanity?
- Others do not approve of me?
- I am sued?
- I'm mistakenly accused of a crime.
- I have a conflict with coworker?
- I never marry?
- I can't get pregnant?
- My boss doesn't like me?

- My work doesn't meet standards?
- A loved one or I contract a foreign virus or other serious illness like cancer?
- This plane gets highjacked or crashes?
- Social Security is inadequate?
- My spouse wants a divorce?
- I become a victim of road rage?
- I become disabled?
- My fear turns into a phobia?
- I am betrayed?
- I start doubting God?
- I don't live up to my potential?

All such worry is useless—we cannot know the future—yet we do it anyway. Worry distracts, is illogical, leads to indecisiveness, and helps no one. It just causes grief. All of us worry, even the disciples of Jesus. Can't you just hear the "what-ifs" they must have thought when Jesus rode into Jerusalem on a donkey? *What if someone attacks or arrests Jesus or us? What if we are prevented from returning to our families? What if Jesus is thrown into prison or even killed—what will happen to us? What if this crowd gets unruly?*

We call an exaggerated or habitual worry a *phobia.* Phobias are irrational, but they're very real to the person suffering from them. A list of over 500 known phobias is displayed on *phobialist.com.* Sometimes you wonder what kind of people make up these phobias, such as "Luposlipaphobia"—the fear of being pursued by timber wolves around a kitchen table while wearing socks on a freshly waxed floor! *Changethatsrightnow.com* advertises: "Your Phobia. Gone. Guaranteed." A one-time fee of only $985 will buy you one or more face-to-face or telephone sessions as needed to get peace of mind (emphasis on "one" session).

Worry has been likened to trying to go somewhere by revving the car engine in neutral. It's not until you put in it gear that anything happens. Entertainer Glenn Yarbrough used to sing, "Worry's like a rocking chair, you go back and forth but you get nowhere."

Every so often we hear of tragic mistakes or situations and worry they may happen to us. For example,

- Sixteen-year-old Jessica Santillan received a heart and lung transplant that did not match her blood type. She later died as a result.
- Told she had an aggressive form of cancer, Linda McDougal consented to a double mastectomy, only to discover later that she did not have cancer.
- City officials and shop owners are

concerned about the overflowing banks
of the Fanda-Menta canal in Venice,
Italy, which threatens its tourist trade
and survival. Engineers have proposed a
plan, which they hope will solve the
problem.

Things like this happen in life, but they need
not cause us to worry. Positive anxiety or concern
may motivate us to realize we need to be an
active advocate for our own health care issues in
order to prevent such mistakes. Worry just paralyzes us. The people in Venice are concerned
about this huge problem but are doing something constructive to solve it, not just sitting in
their rocking chairs and saying, "What if?"

People often quote ten words spoken by former
President Franklin Roosevelt regarding fear: "The
only thing we have to fear is fear itself."
However, the full meaning doesn't surface until
we read the rest of the sentence: "The only thing
we have to fear is fear itself—nameless, unreason-
ing, unjustified terror which paralyzes needed
efforts to convert retreat into advance."[4]

Erect a "No Trespassing" sign

What can we do to unlearn fear-filled thought
patterns that trouble us so and stand tall to the
"what-ifs" of life? First, when tempted to worry,

try erecting a "No Trespassing" sign in your mind. Try to visualize it facing the worry that attempts to capture your thoughts. Remind yourself of three things:

1. Worry is sin.
2. Worry wastes valuable time.
3. Nothing positive comes from worry.

These statements are value judgments. Norm Wright says, "Unless we make a value judgment on our negative behavior, we will never change."[5] Wright claims many people like to worry. They've practiced it so long it's a way of life.

At Mount Ebal, Moses set forth potential blessings and curses for Israel, depending upon whether or not they refused to follow the Lord's ways. He describes one of the curses as an "anxious mind":

> There the Lord will give you an anxious mind, eyes weary with longing, and a despairing heart. You will live in constant suspense, filled with dread both night and day, never sure of your life. (Deuteronomy 28:65–66, NIV)

In this passage the Hebrew word used for "anxious" *(raggaz)* expresses frenzy stemming from a deeper emotion which may manifest itself in trembling. It also refers to the earth quaking.

One of my most fearful experiences occurred when I was a very young boy and my Mom and I visited my grandmother in Nebraska. One stormy evening I heard the town siren crank up. Afraid, I asked my grandmother what it meant and she said, "Someone has spotted a tornado nearby." I was too young to now recall the details, but I do remember starting to cry and shaking uncontrollably with fear. That's what *raggaz* means.

I don't know how long the warning lasted, but until it was over I was a wreck. I remember clinging to my mother the entire time and her trying to comfort me. I'm sure my little mind wondered, *What if we get hurt? What if we get killed?* Fear of the unknown paralyzed me.

The tornado never came. Now tornadoes intrigue me—I even chased one with some other college friends one time. Why I reacted that earlier way remains a mystery, but *raggaz* totally consumed my young mind.

In Proverbs 12:25, Solomon states that a worrisome or anxious mind weighs down one's spirit. The antidote is a kind word spoken by a friend to cheer him up. This word indicates a state of mind leading to fear. Ezekiel uses the same word *(d'agah)* to describe the kind of worries that will afflict people when Jerusalem's enemies seize her, namely anxiety over the supply of food (Ezekiel 4:16; 12:19).

The most often used New Testament word for worry or anxiety *(merimna, merimnao)* occurs eighty percent of the time in a negative sense, but it can also be translated "care" or "to care" signifying a genuine concern. The mind is pulled in different directions or distracted from ordinary matters to the circumstance that troubles the mind, either positively (care) or negatively (worry).

Jesus tells us not to worry about the basic provisions of life but to trust God to provide: "do not worry. . . . your heavenly Father knows that you need them" (Matthew 6:25, 32, NIV). Trusting involves seeking to pattern our lives after kingdom principles: "Seek first his kingdom and his righteousness and all these things will be given to you as well. Therefore, do not worry about tomorrow, for tomorrow will worry about itself. Each day has enough trouble of its own" (6:33–34, NIV).

Commenting on this passage, Carol Kent writes, "That must mean that worrying about things that haven't happened yet is a direct act of disobedience. God says every day that comes my way will have plenty of its own trauma, and I'm not to dwell on future 'what ifs.'"[6] Jeremiah describes the condition of a person who trusts in the Lord:

> But blessed is the man who trusts in
> the Lord, whose confidence is in him.
> He will be like a tree planted by the
> water. . . . It has no worries in a year of
> drought. (Jeremiah 17:7–8, NIV)

Erecting a "No Trespassing" sign will help you stand tall against worry's stranglehold.

Have a little talk with Jesus

I know it dates me, but a pleasant memory from one of the churches I served relates to hearing the men's quartet sing an old song, "Just a little talk with Jesus." One of their signature songs, it reminded us of prayer's importance.

Besides erecting that sign, we also need to have a little talk with Jesus when faced with worries. The psalmists wrote much about worry and anxiety, often in the form of a prayer:

> When anxiety was great within me,
> your consolation brought joy to my soul.
> (Psalm 94:19, NIV)

> Search me, O God, and know my
> heart; test me and know my anxious

thoughts. (Psalm 139:23, NIV)

The Hebrew word used for "anxious" and "anxiety" *(sar-appiym)* has the idea of disquieting, troublesome thoughts. In the first case, the writer recounts how God helped him through an anxious time. In the second verse, David asks God to bring to his mind worries that needed cleansing.

In his challenge to church leaders, the apostle Peter uses the same word for worry we just examined in Matthew 6. He exhorts them to "Cast all your anxiety *(merimnan)* on him because he cares for you" (1 Peter 5:7, NIV). The idea expressed by "cast" is that of throwing off something onto someone or something else, like tossing a blanket or saddle on a horse in order to ride.

To accomplish this task, we must bring ourselves low before the Lord, renouncing any pride that may hinder our prayer: "Humble yourselves, therefore, under the mighty hand of God, that He may exalt you at the proper time" (1 Peter 5:6, NASB). We can trust a caring Lord to shoulder our worries.

In Philippians 4:6–7, the apostle Paul explains how to reduce worry:

> Don't worry about anything, but pray about everything. With thankful hearts

> offer up your prayers and requests to
> God. Then, because you belong to Christ
> Jesus, God will bless you with peace that
> no one can completely understand. And
> this peace will control the way you think
> and feel. (CEV)

This verse teaches that a peaceful mind comes from trusting prayer. Bring every worry to his attention and throw it upon him (from 1 Peter 5:7) and God promises to "control the way you think and feel," or to "guard our hearts and minds" (NIV) against that particular troublesome fear as we stand in Jesus.

The way to make this work, however, is in a little phrase we often bypass— "with thankful hearts," or "with thanksgiving" (NIV). One of the most helpful books I've read on worry is Donald Baker's *Thank You Therapy.* He emphasizes the thanksgiving part of this passage as the key that unlocks the door to peace. We present the anxiety to God, and then thank him for hearing us, caring about us, and handling the situation in his way and time.

We need to channel all the energy we spend worrying into praying. Greg Laurie offers a sample prayer:

Lord, here is my problem. It bothers me. It has not gone away. It looms ever larger in my path. Thus, I am putting it in your hands. I'm not going to worry, Lord. I am going to trust you. I'm even going to thank you in advance that you know what you are doing. And you will work it out for your own glory.[7]

Now if you're like me, that worry tends to re-enter my mind during the day, so what do we do then? It won't work to "cast" that care upon him again (1 Peter 5:7, NIV), for if that's all we do we'll just feel the same or worse. The tense of that word "cast" denotes a one-time action, not to be repeated.

We're to simply thank him again that he now has the worry. He loves to "worry" for us! As often as that fear raises its ugly head during the day, face it head-on by thanking him. A common phrase I use to stand tall against repeating fears is "Thank you for the victory that lies ahead." There's something about thanking him that brings on that "peace . . . which surpasses all comprehension" (NASB), and that something is faith.

Someone may be thinking, "Isn't having to thank him over and over a lack of faith?" No. To keep begging him would indicate weak faith, but to *thank* him encourages growth in faith, because we remind ourselves of his promise in Philippians 4 to bring about a victory of peace: "Faith comes from hearing, and hearing by the word of Christ" (Romans 10:17, NASB). Prominent physician and psychiatrist Paul Tournier wrote, "The Christian is not exempt from fear, but he takes his fears to God. Faith does not suppress fear; what it does is to allow one to go forward in spite of it."[8]

One more thing—do you realize that when you pray, that prayer also fits in with God's overall plan for the future? He uses our prayers to change things and people. As Richard Foster says, when we pray "we are working with God to determine the future!"[9]

As we make a habit out of taking our worries to the Lord in prayer, we learn through his Word and his still small voice to listen for his instructions in how to deal with the matter at hand.

Get his promises down pat

Not only do we need to erect a "No Trespassing" sign and have a little talk with Jesus, but we also must *get his promises down pat.* The famous conductor Arturo Toscanini memorized every note for every musical instrument in 250 symphonies and 100 operas. This stored-up information enabled him to direct his pieces with practically flawless ability. It's important to base everything we do on God's Word. Memorizing Scripture helps us focus on God, rather than our fears.

Someone shared a simple tool with me years ago to help control troublesome thoughts. I simply wrote out Philippians 4:8–9 on one side of a 3x5 card. On the other side I wrote in large letters, "STOP!" Whenever a worry threatened, I would take the card out of my shirt pocket, actually say, "STOP," and meditate on the verses which point the way to a more positive pattern of thinking:

> Fix your thoughts on what is true and honorable and right. Think about things that are pure and lovely and admirable. Think about things that are excellent and worthy of praise. Keep putting into practice all you learned from me and heard from me and saw me doing, and the God of peace will be with you. ()

You might want to learn the suggested memory passage for this week, Philippians 4:6–9, in the same way by adding verses six and seven. Memorized scripture allows the Holy Spirit to bring God's calming word to our minds, and he reassures us of his presence and power. As we recall verses and passages, God often tells us the appropriate actions to take.

One time a meeting scheduled a month away caused me much anxiety. So, rather than sweat it out for the next thirty days I decided to at least try reducing my anxiety by memorizing Psalm 121 in which God presents himself as our source of strength and protection. I also made a list of possible consequences from that meeting, from the worst case scenario to the best possible outcome. Then I rated the probabilities, which helped reduce my fears. Each time a worrisome thought came to me I read over the Psalm (eventually quoting it) and reviewed the card. This process helped me live a more normal life and not lose so much of my joy by worrying.

A notable scene in *The Lord of the Rings* has Lady Galadriel inviting Sam to look into a basin of water called the Mirror of Galadriel. To the onlooker it reveals the past, present, and future. Wanting to know about the situation back in the Shire, Sam agrees. In the mirror he sees disturbing scenes, like hobbits mercilessly cutting down trees that were meant to grow, and old buildings being destroyed.

Sam pulls away from the Mirror in despair,

vowing to return at once to correct the wrongs. Then, Galadriel reminds him of his pledge to stay with Frodo, and bids him remember that because the Mirror shows things that have not yet happened or may never happen, it is an unreliable guide to the future.[10] Sam chooses to stay.

The Word of God is our only reliable guide. As we practice erecting "No Trespassing" signs, having little talks with Jesus, and getting his promises down pat, we can expect to see meaningful changes in our relationship with life's fears. Be patient, because learning to live without a fear requires adjustment in the way we think. Remember Jesus' words to live one day at a time:

> Therefore, do not worry about tomorrow, for tomorrow will worry about itself. Each day has enough trouble of its own. (Matthew 6:34, NIV)

This short poem, "My Name is 'I AM,'" by Helen Callicoat, teaches us to take life day by day:

> *I was regretting the past and fearing the*
> *future.*
> *Suddenly, I heard God speaking.*
> *"My name is 'I AM.'"*
> *He paused. I waited.*

He continued, "When you live in the past
with its mistakes and regrets, it is hard for
you because I am not there.
"My name is not 'I WAS.'
"When you live in the future with its
unknowns and fears, it is hard for you
because I am not there.
"My name is not 'I WILL BE.'
"But when you live in this moment, it is
not hard, because I am here.
My name is 'I AM.'"

And because he is the I AM, we can stand
tall—fearful, but unafraid.

[1] H. Norman Wright, *Afraid No More* (Wheaton, IL: Tyndale
House Publishers, 1989) 130.

[2] Charles Mayo, quoted in Greg Laurie, *Why Believe?*
(Wheaton, IL: Tyndale House Publishers, Inc., 2002) 36.

[3] Told by Don McCullough.

[4] Franklin Delano Roosevelt, First Inaugural Address, 4 March
1933.

[5] H. N. Wright 139.

[6] Carol Kent, *Tame Your Fears* (Colorado Springs, CO:
NavPress, 2003) 70.

[7] Laurie 48.

[8] Paul Tournier, *The Strong and the Weak* (Philadelphia:
Westminster, 1963) 93.

[9] Richard Foster, *Celebration of Discipline* (San Francisco:
HarperCollins, 1988) 35.

[10] J. R. R. Tolkien, *The Fellowship of the Ring* (Boston:
Houghton Mifflin Company, 1994) 353–354.

The eyes of the Lord
watch over those who do right,
his ears are open to their cries for help.
—*Psalm 34:15*

chapter eight

loosening the grip of
gathering doom

Knowing where you are going takes
the uncertainty out of getting there.
—Anne Graham Lotz

What fear inside you keeps you from living to the fullest?" Lloyd Ogilvie, former Chaplain of the U.S. Senate, has asked people this question over the years. Of the thousands of responses, *fear of the future* ranked among the top six answers.[1]

Many believers fear what we may have to go through before living with Christ in heaven.

Some are so terrified of the future that they don't want to have children in such times. We don't like the way the country and world are headed, and what we may have to endure makes us anxious. We fear that which we can't control or that we feel we can't control. Some of the issues bothering believers concern declining moral values, global warming, our culture of anxiety, nuclear proliferation, weapons of mass destruction, and the end of civilization as we know it. How difficult it must be for non-Christians in today's world.

Harvard professor Samuel P. Huntington rings a warning bell when he says, "On a world-wide basis Civilization seems in many respects to be yielding to barbarism, generating the image of an unprecedented phenomenon, a global Dark Ages, possibly descending on humanity."[2]

In *Till Armageddon!,* written in 1981, Billy Graham reflects: "The whole world is sighing and suffering on a scale perhaps not known in human history. . . . It seems that the human race may well be heading toward the climax of the tears, hurts and wounds of the centuries—Armageddon!"[3]

The world did not appear that way to me in 1981. My attention centered more on finishing

and paying for a new church facility, transition-
ing our congregation fives miles down the road,
and then filling our new twice-as-large worship
center, among other things of life and ministry.
Since then events like the terrorist attack on the
Marines barracks in Lebanon (1983); the Berlin
Wall's destruction (1989); the dissolution of the
USSR (1991); terrorist attacks on the World
Trade Center (1993, 2001), on the Pentagon,
and on another (attempted) Washington, D.C.
target (2001); plus the military campaigns in
Afghanistan and Iraq have increasingly grabbed
more of my attention and heightened my
concern.

Have world conditions worsened? It would
seem so.

According to a Barna Research Group survey,
moral decline is an important concern mostly
among Christians but also among a significant
percentage of non-Christians. Particular issues
noted include substance abuse, crime, violence,
spiritual decay, loss of family values, and general
discomfort regarding the moral climate. Issues
that did not get high marks were homosexuality,
abortion, cloning, child abuse, and pornography.
The Barna Group could not ascertain whether
respondents' lack of concern was due to being

burned out on the issue, not understanding it, or just not holding a position either way.[5]

In *Boiling Point,* researcher George Barna lists fourteen facts of life not at all up for grabs two generations ago that have changed in the twenty-first century:[6]

- Men proposed marriage to women.
- Children were educated in schools.
- Men ran corporations and the government.
- The courts would uphold existing legislation rather than create new laws.
- People would respect authority figures, such as clergy, the president of the country, police officers or military officials.
- Individuals would honor their contracts.
- The mass media would honor traditional norms of decency.
- Lawsuits were a means of last recourse.
- Banks never went bankrupt.
- National heroes were upstanding citizens.
- Americans appreciated their country and respected its symbols, such as the flag and national anthem.
- Public courtesy was the norm.

Change will occur in the future, but there's nothing we can do to change the future. As a result, we live in tension, wanting certain things never to change, yet forced to face the changes that are present and real. As one writer stated it, we're like a paper clip in the middle of two equally powerful magnets.[7] Our inability to know for certain what will happen makes us nervous, fearful, and anxious for ourselves and those we love.

Live today

Many identify with Tolkien's assessment of the warring times in which he lived, as expressed through his Middle Earthen characters. In a conversation with Gandalf, Frodo Baggins laments the return of the Dark Lord to power and wishes it had not happened during his lifetime. Gandalf agrees that the future looks bleak and that many others in Middle Earth feel the same.

But then he states something vitally important to those of us who feel the same about the twenty-first century: "All we have to decide is what to do with the time that is given us."[8] No one offered us the choice of when to live. Our parents had no choice in the matter, either. God made that decision; thus, our task is not to lament over the decline of our world but to make wise use of the time we have as a gift.

Somewhere I ran across a bit of wisdom worded something like this: "Live as if today were your last day, but plan as if you'll be around for a long time." This truth comes through powerfully in a 1993 film entitled *Groundhog Day,* which I saw for the first time recently. Most of the story takes place in Punxsutawney, Pennsylvania, on "Groundhog Day," when a groundhog named "Punxsutawney Phil" annually forecasts whether the nation will have six weeks more of winter weather.

A television station in Pittsburgh sends its ace weatherman, Phil Conners, to do a remote broadcast on the Groundhog Festival, especially the part where the animal sees his shadow or not. Conners is an egotistic "prima donna" who hates this yearly assignment and dislikes everything about Punxsutawney, including the people. He fully expects to do the report and head back to Pittsburgh, but a blizzard prevents him and the crew from returning.

Forced to stay another night in his bed and breakfast, the adventure begins. As his alarm awakes him the next morning, he is shocked to discover a repeat of February 2, Groundhog Day. Each morning the same thing happens, day after day, with everything repeating itself for a total of thirty-four days.

All the events on that "second" February 2 are identical to what happened the first day, except for Conners's frame of mind. Confused and upset, he tries an experiment before retiring for the night. He breaks a pencil and lays it on the nightstand. The next morning, however, he finds the pencil unbroken, and hears the same music playing. The same disc jockeys pass along the identical weather forecast that Conners heard yesterday and the day before, and the same announcement concerning Groundhog Day.

Soon, Conners begins to like this change of pace. Living the same day over again gives him an excuse to indulge in vices and do crazy things without any regrets. Tomorrow everything will turn into today again. However, after living recklessly for a while, Conners grows depressed at the realization that some fluke of time has sentenced him to the same people in the same circumstances every day with no hope of a different tomorrow. He attempts suicide a number of times, but each day he wakes up as if it is still February 2.

Eventually Conners decides to make the most of each day by doing something to improve himself. So, he takes piano lessons, creates ice sculptures, and learns to recite poetry in French. He gets quite good at these things, because his skill improves day after day. He changes, even though the rest of the town doesn't.

Then it occurs to him that he could be helping people, since he knows what has happened to them today and will repeat itself the next day, unless he intervenes. So he saves a man choking on food, catches a boy falling from a tree, fixes a flat tire for three elderly ladies, prevents a couple from ending their engagement, and buys someone food. He changes each one of the outcomes—every day—and gains a great deal of satisfaction from his good deeds.

Suspiciously similar to "It's a Wonderful Life," this process of self-redemption changes Conner into a more thoughtful, considerate, caring person, and he eventually awakens to February 3 on the "35th" day. The time warp forces him to face his weaknesses and make the best of every day by growing into a better person and a more productive member of Punxsutawney where he chooses to settle down.

The Apostle Paul said it first: "Make the most of every opportunity for doing good in these evil days" (Ephesians 5:16). Note that Paul considered his times "evil" as well, and that his solution was to make a difference for the good. Regret over the past and worry over what lies ahead rob today of peace and joy. Life will then be, as former Beatle John Lennon wrote, "what happens to you while you're busy making other plans."

Jesus told his disciples, "Peace I leave with you; my peace I give you. I do not give to you as the world gives. Do not let your hearts be troubled and do not be afraid" (John 14:27, NIV). He didn't promise that conditions would improve, only that his disciples need not fear because he would give them peace amidst the turmoil. He promised that even though fearful of the future we can face it unafraid.

Until he returns, the Lord also promises protection: "The eyes of the Lord watch over those who do right; his ears are open to their cries for help" (Psalm 34:15). Ours is a God who keeps watch over his children, like a parent who checks on the kids at night to see if they are sleeping and well. Unlike parents, the Lord "never tires and never sleeps" (Psalm 121:4). He's always by our side as a protective shade from evil, watching over us as we come and go (Psalm 121:5–8).

The Shepherd Psalm reinforces this promise: "Surely goodness and unfailing love will pursue me all the days of my life, and I will dwell in the house of the Lord forever" (Psalm 23:6). This verse promises that our good and mercifully loving God unrelentingly sticks with us through thick and thin. "Pursue" or "follow" is elsewhere used in Scripture to mean a hunter's tenacity in tracking his prey. In like manner, the Lord is our unfailing constant companion.

Because of his goodness, we can expect him to work out all things that happen to us—including the bad things that happen to good people—for our ultimate good and His glory. Commenting on a similar passage, Romans 8:28, Ogilvie writes,

> He is constantly working to increase our joys and strengthen us in our difficulties. . . . That's the confidence that cures fear of the future. We are promised neither a trouble-free future nor one in which things will eventually work out. What we are promised is that God will work all things together with creative continuity for our ultimate good. Tomorrow is under His control. . . . God knows what He's doing! He's with us in Christ.[9]

His "unfailing love" or "mercy" follows us as well. He pardons and forgives our missteps off the path because Jesus Christ has taken upon himself the guilt for those sins. One of the richest Hebrew words, it has no adequate equivalent in

English. Try putting the concepts of mercy, kind-ness, love, lovingkindness, loyalty, compassion, and fidelity into one English word and you will understand God's heart and mind toward his sheep.

In Psalm 84, the psalmist reveals that his pre-dominant desire in life is to live where God lives. His reason? "Blessed are those who dwell in your house; they are ever praising you" (verse 4, NIV). These are King David's sentiments exactly, for he closes Psalm 23 with the same thought. The apostle Paul agrees:

> Our bodies are like tents that we live in here on earth. But when these tents are destroyed, we know that God will give each of us a place to live. These homes will not be buildings that someone has made, but they are in heaven and will last forever (2 Corinthians 5:1, CEV).

Forever is a long time—a lot longer than these short years on earth. All of us will live forever in one of two real places—heaven or hell. Heaven waits for all who place their trust in Jesus Christ for eternal life for forgiveness from sin. In Colossians 2:13–15, Paul explains that when Christ sacrificed his life on the cross, he made cleansing possible for all our sins—past, present, and future.

We need forgiveness because all are spiritually dead without Christ. The bill with our name on it that says, "Guilty," Jesus nailed to his cross, canceling the charges by paying the debt for us. By doing so, he also divested himself of the evil powers that tempted him to disobey his Father, winning the battle and claiming victory by shaming them publicly.

Because Christ rose from the dead, those who trust him "live with a wonderful expectation," writes the apostle Peter (1 Peter 1:3). That expectation involves:

1. An imperishable inheritance: "an inheritance that can never perish, spoil or fade—kept in heaven for you" (1 Peter 1:4, NIV). This gift may be what Isaiah meant when he said the Messiah would "divide the spoils with the many" (53:12, NIV). It includes eternal life with Christ and being renewed in knowledge and in his image (Colossians 3:10, paraphrased): Each of you is now a new person. You are becoming more and more like your Creator, and you will understand him better.

2. God's protective power in the mean time to

guard the faith we have in him: "And God, in his mighty power, will protect you until you receive this salvation, because you are trusting him" (1 Peter 1:5, NLT); and "Guard the good deposit that was entrusted to you—guard it with the help of the Holy Spirit who lives in us" (2 Timothy 1:14, NIV).

3. Necessary trials to refine, strengthen, and prove our faith genuine: "So be truly glad! There is wonderful joy ahead, even though it is necessary for you to endure many trials for a while. These trials are only to test your faith, to show that it is strong and pure. It is being tested as fire tests and purifies gold—and your faith is far more precious to God than mere gold" (1 Peter 1:6–7).

4. Praise, glory, and honor on the day Jesus reveals himself to the world: "So if your faith remains strong after being tried by fiery trials, it will bring you much praise and glory and honor on the day when Jesus Christ is revealed to the whole world" (1 Peter 1:7).

Jesus said that just before he returns, instability in the heavens and on earth will produce turmoil and cause people to lose their courage. Whatever cause they may attach to these events, people will be terribly afraid of the unknown outcome.

Then, Christ will come again: "everyone will see the Son of Man arrive on the clouds with power and great glory" (Luke 21:27). Those who love and trust Christ need not have fear, for it is our Savior who comes to reign. Jesus says to the believers, "So when all these things begin to happen, stand straight and look up, for your salvation is near!" (Luke 21:28). It will be a time of great rejoicing for the friends of Christ!

Anticipate your joy when Jesus is revealed

After the Ring and Mount Doom's power is destroyed, the time arrives for the rightful king to claim the throne of Gondor. Frodo carries the crown and Gandalf places it upon the head of the kneeling Aragorn. As the new king—now called Elessar—stands, light encompasses him. Those nearby perceive him as tall, wise, ancient of days, with strong hands ready to protect and heal. The steward, Faramir, cries out, "Behold the King!" Trumpets begin to blow as the new king walks through beautiful streets accompanied by music, singing, rejoicing, and laughter. The doom is no more.[10]

When our Lord Jesus Christ—Light of the

world, King of kings, Ancient of days, all-wise, all-powerful, our Refuge and Healer—is revealed, the joy will be unparalleled. In anticipation of His return, the apostle John gives us a preview:

> Then I heard again what sounded like the shout of a huge crowd, or the roar of mighty ocean waves, or the crash of loud thunder: "Hallelujah! For the Lord our God, the Almighty, reigns. Let us be glad and rejoice and honor him" . . . Then I saw heaven opened, and a white horse was standing there. And the one sitting on the horse was named Faithful and True. For he judges fairly and then goes to war. His eyes were bright like flames of fire and on his head were many crowns. . . . On his robe and thigh was written this title: King of kings and Lord of lords. (Revelation 19:6–7a, 11–12a, 16)

One practical way we can stand tall against the gloom of gathering doom is to start making a list of the things that will be cause for joy when Jesus returns. Get a sheet of paper and write on the top: "What I'm going to be joyous about on that day when Jesus Christ is revealed to the whole world." Or, you might want to approach it this way by writing, "As a follower of Jesus Christ, I stand tall against the fear of gathering doom. When I think about Jesus appearing to the whole world, I anticipate feeling very joyous for the following reasons. . . ."

When I made my list and reviewed it, one thing towered above the others. I wrote: "Just finally seeing him face to face." When Jesus appears, I will see a perfect Lord—perfect in love, holiness, fairness, righteousness, goodness, strength, knowledge, and so on. My thoughts turned toward songs written about seeing Christ. I love many of the contemporary worship songs, but the lyrics in some of the old hymns are rich with meaning. Thumbing through an old hymnal for a few minutes revealed some joyous anticipations:

It will be worth it all when we see Jesus,
Life's trials will seem so small when we see
  Christ. ("When We See Christ")

When we all see Jesus,
We'll sing and shout the victory. ("When*
  We All Get to Heaven")

When by His grace I shall look on His face,
That will be glory, be glory for me!
  ("O That Will Be Glory")

Face to face with my Redeemer,
Jesus Christ who loves me so!

("Face to Face")

And I shall see Him face to face,
And tell the story—Saved by grace.
  ("Saved by Grace")

Your list may uncover a different aspect of joy
at our Lord's revelation, but whatever you jot
down, when you do this exercise something else
starts to happen. When we choose to reflect on
the joy we anticipate experiencing when Jesus is
revealed, we will not only increase our expectation for that day, but the whole contemplative
process enhances the joy we sense in the present
moment.

Did you just notice how I described my
thoughts concerning the joy of finally seeing
Jesus? As I located those songs I began to praise
God by singing some of those verses. The antici-
pated joy of that *future* experience affects me
today, even right now. I began by making a list
and then envisioned his return. As I meditated,
joy started bubbling up like a pot of water
approaching the boiling point. And that joy I feel
now affects this hour of my life, and the gathering doom—of the world, or my personal
world—doesn't seem so dark and ominous.

A story told by Maria Hanna concerns two

birds and how they reacted to adverse conditions. Each bird, used to flying free, was put into its own cage and supplied with ample food and water. One bird was very unhappy, refusing to eat or drink, and banged its head against the cage door. In just a few hours, it died. The other bird thought, "Nothing's worth dying that way. Let me enjoy the food and water and be grateful for the little space in which I can fly." At the end of the day, the master came to free the birds. Only one of them could rejoice at seeing its master.

The truly free bird enjoyed the life granted to it and eventually found freedom. Eugene Petersen's *The Message* communicates the kind of attitude that stands tall against the fears that grip our souls:

> That's why we live with such good cheer. You won't see us drooping our heads or dragging our feet! Cramped conditions here don't get us down. They only remind us of the spacious living conditions ahead. It's what we trust in but don't yet see that keeps us going. Do you suppose a few ruts in the road or rocks in the path are going to stop us? When the time comes, we'll be plenty ready to exchange exile for homecoming.

But neither exile nor homecoming is the main thing. Cheerfully pleasing God is the main thing, and that's what we aim to do, regardless of our conditions. Sooner or later we'll all have to face God, regardless of our conditions. We will appear before Christ and take what's coming to us as a result of our actions, either good or bad (2 Corinthians 5:6–10).

[1] Lloyd John Ogilvie, *Facing the Future Without Fear* (Ann Arbor, MI: Vine Books, 2002) 20.

[2] Samuel P. Huntington, *The Clash of Civilizations and The Remaking of World Order* (New York: A Touchstone Book, Simon & Schuster, 1997) 321.

[3] Billy Graham, *Till Armageddon!* (Minneapolis, MN: Grason, 1981) 7.

[4] Anne Graham Lotz, *Heaven: My Father's House* (Nashville: W Publishing Group, 2001) viii.

[5] *Barna Research Online,* 26 March 2002, <barna.org>.

[6] George Barna, *Boiling Point* (Ventura, CA: Regal Books, 2001) 19.

[7] Gerald L. Sittser, *The Will of God as a Way of Life* (Grand Rapids: Zondervan Publishing House, 2000) 149.

[8] J. R. R. Tolkien, *The Fellowship of the Ring* (Boston: Houghton Mifflin Company, 1994) 50.

[9] Lloyd John Ogilvie, *Lord of the Impossible* (Nashville: Abingdon, 1984) 190.

[10] Tolkien, *The Return of the King* (Boston: Houghton Mifflin, 1994) 946–947.

Discover the presence of God in your life!

Join Karen Mains on the God Hunt—a playful and profound way to seek and find those seemingly ordinary moments when God intervenes in your life with guidance, care, and help.

You'll find it happens more often than you think! And you'll be drawn into deeper communion with God as you "tune in" to the many ways he answers prayer, shows evidence of his love, helps you do his work in the world, and "works all things together for good."

First developed by Karen and David Mains as a teaching tool for their children, the God Hunt has since been used by thousands of churchgoers worldwide.

"Karen writes, 'It is a sin to make the Christian life boring.' The same may be true for Christian books. This one is anything but—a wise, literate, concrete guide to spiritual life."

—John Ortberg, author of
If You Want to Walk on Water, You've Got to Get Out of the Boat

For information on how you can order *The God Hunt* and other resources from Mainstay, call toll-free 1-800-224-2735 or visit our website at www.sundaysolutions.com.